Canada's Kids

Books by Sabra Holbrook

The French Founders of North America and Their Heritage
Lafayette: Man in the Middle
Growing Up in France
Canada's Kids

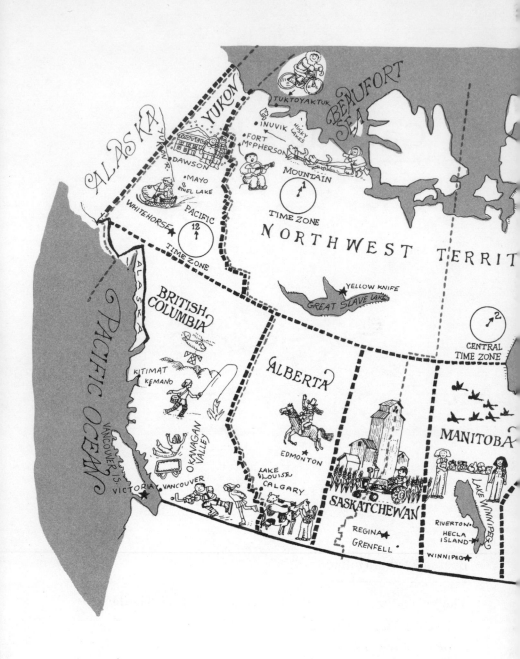

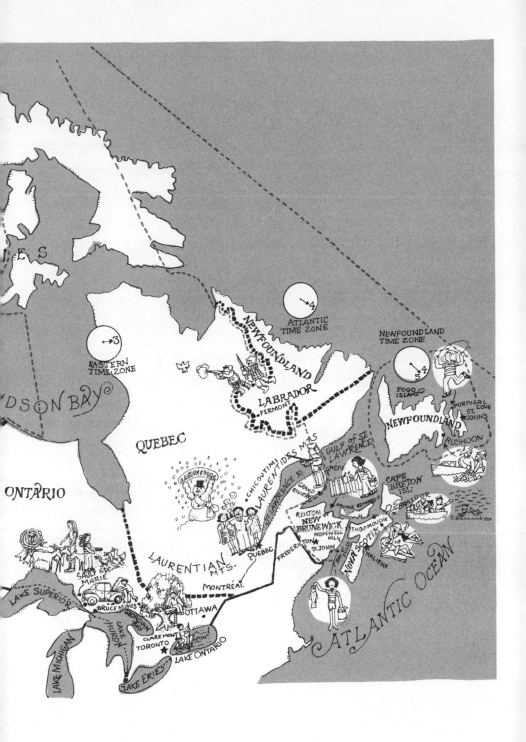

Canada's Kids

by SABRA HOLBROOK

Illustrated with photographs and map

Atheneum 1983 New York

LIBRARY OF CONGRESS CATALOGING IN PUBLICATION DATA

Holbrook, Sabra.   Canada's kids.

  Bibliography: p. 136
  Includes index.
  SUMMARY: The author reports on Canada through
the eyes of Canadian young people with whom she
lived for seven months in rural, urban, and suburban
areas and in Eskimo and Indian villages.
  1. Children—Canada—Social conditions—
Juvenile literature. 2. Children—Canada—Case
studies—Juvenile literature. 3. Children—
Canada—Attitudes—Juvenile literature. [1. Canada
—Social life and customs] I. Title.
HQ792.C3H64 1983   305.2'3'0971   83-6355
ISBN 0-689-31002-1

Copyright © 1983 by Sabra Holbrook
All rights reserved
Published simultaneously in Canada by
McClelland & Stewart, Ltd.
Text set by Maryland Linotype, Baltimore, Maryland
Printed and bound
by Fairfield Graphics, Fairfield, Pennsylvania
Designed by Marjorie Zaum
First Edition

For an Indomitable Canadian
SAM WALKER

Acknowledgments

I SHOULD FIRST OF ALL LIKE TO ACKNOWLEDGE MY DEBT TO THE boys and girls and parents whose names appear in this book. Without their warm hospitality and willingness to supply whatever information I sought, the book simply could not have been written.

Next, my thanks are due to all those who made my home-stays and other close experiences with children possible. They include: the secretaries of Canadian farm and/or country vacation associations in the various provinces, all of whom were most diligent in helping me locate families of varying backgrounds; also to the Right Reverend John T. Frame, Bishop of the Anglican Diocese of the Yukon; the Right Reverend John R. Sperry, Bishop of the Arctic; the Reverend Donald J. Lawton, Anglican Church of Canada, Elsa, Yukon; the Reverend Dan Meakes, Rector, Saint Paul's Church, Dawson City, Yukon; the Reverend J. A. Yorke, Saint John's Anglican Mission, Tuktoyaktuk, Northwest Territories; Dr.

Acknowledgments

Arthur M. Sullivan, Mr. G. Bruce Woodland of Newfoundland's Memorial University, Mr. Richard Straus who sent me to them; Mr. Dennis Cichelly and Mrs. Margaret Hawkins of Inuvik, Northwest Territories; Mr. Roy L. Sewer, of Saint John, U.S. Virgin Islands (who, in his capacity as Lions' Club President, contacted Mr. Cichelly, Inuvik Lions' Club President, on my behalf), Mr. Sam Walker, Mr. Christopher Thomson, Agent de Recherche, Direction des Communications, Québec; Mr. and Mrs Peter Weissner, Thornhill, British Columbia; Mme. Louise Tremblay, Chicoutimi, Québec, her grandson, Ian Cyr, and her sister Mlle. Madeleine Smith.

I am grateful for further enlightenment on the Québec-federal relationship to an old and deeply respected friend, M. Claude Morin, Minister of Intergovernmental Affairs for the Province of Québec.

I owe a great many thanks to officials in the field of education, especially M. André Pardoën and M. Claude Bernard in the Québec Ministry of Education, Mme. Diane Lapierre, of the Service des Étudiants de la Commission des Écoles Catholiques de Québec, Mme. Henriette Robadey, and M. Robert Ascah of Montréal's Commission des Ecoles Catholiques, Mr. Ron Patterson of Montréal's Protestant Schools.

Also to the following school directors: M. Michel Lanctôt and Sister Simon Beaudoin, Fermont; M. Claude Miniville, Grand Rivière; M. Jean-Paul Fournier and Sister Marie Bouchard, Gaspé, in Québec, Mme. Rachel Audet, in Montréal, M. Emile Robichaud and Miss Mona Macnab; in West Toronto, Mrs. Barbara Synnestvedt; in Claremont, Mr. Richard Hanna; in Hopewell Hill, Mr. Reginald Duffy.

Further, I am most appreciative of opportunities given me by classroom teachers whose name appear in this book for chances to observe their classes and talk with their students.

Acknowledgments

For information on forest care my thanks go to Mr. Rhikaillo and Doug Flintoft of Woodlands, and to Mr. and Mrs. Ernest Vaissiere, who introduced me to Woodlands. I am also grateful for the courtesy extended to me at Kemano by Mr. Colin Tabbiner and Mr. Frank Armitage.

Finally, another person without whose help this book would not have appeared is Mrs. Lee Hennessy, my long-time typist, with patience equal to her skill.

S. H.

A Word About This Book

THE DOZENS OF CANADIAN BOYS AND GIRLS WHOM READERS will meet in this book are flesh-and-blood children, doing in the book what they do in their daily lives. The author has many times visited in Canada and has written four previous books about that country. But during the seven months spent in field research for this book, she was not a visitor. She became a member of families, living in children's homes. She went to school with them, camped with them, fished with them, cooked with them, took trips with them, picnicked with them, played their games and celebrated their holidays. She has flown with bush pilots into deep wilderness communities, helped harvest grain in the prairies, mastered the art of eating with chopsticks in a Chinese home, surveyed reindeer herds and tramped through Arctic summer mud in *mukluks*. This is her report on Canada through the eyes of boys and girls with whom she had the privilege of becoming a friend.

A Word About This Book

Readers will meet them first in an overview of their varied life-styles, then through closeups of isolated settlements, thriving towns and big city as well as rural schools. Finally, the picture swings across the vast sweep of the country, stopping with a family in each province from the Maritimes that border the Atlantic to British Columbia on the Pacific.

Contents

CHAPTER **1**

People of the
Many Canadas

RODNEY RADDI, A TEN-YEAR-OLD ESKIMO BOY, RIDES HIS BIKE IN full sunlight at midnight in July along the muddy, main street of Tuktoyaktuk—Tuk, for short—his Canadian Arctic village. He steers as crookedly as a drunk. He isn't. He is, rather, an expert. He's avoiding the ridges and ruts, humps and bumps, made by permafrost.

Permafrost is frozen ground, most of which never melts. Only the top layer softens in summer, turning to mud as gooey as chewing gum. When this layer refreezes in winter, it expands. It can't expand into the ice below, so it swells up instead. In winter, the swollen mounds may be ten feet high. Those Rodney is steering around have melted into mere oozy mudhills.

His nighttime sun results from the tilt of the earth in relation to sunlight. The tilt differs according to season and location. In the high Arctic, the sun shines night and day in

Ivan Emberley, of Rushoon,
waits with the other boys
outside the fish processing plant
for discards.

summer, but winter is almost one long night. This arrange-
ment suits Rodney. He has never known any other. The seasons bring him their own rewards.

In the spring, he can fish for his favorite Arctic char, a
delicacy that combines the color and taste of salmon with
the texture of swordfish. He can hunt caribou for tender
steaks and tough skins. The skins make fine boots. In summer
his father takes him whaling or seal hunting. The groups of
hunters travel in big canoes. The outcome of the search is
important to Rodney's community. The seal gives both meat
and clothing. The whale provides meat, oil, fat and bones
for carving miniature statues that sell for a good price.

In winter Rodney searches snowdrifts for white Arctic
hare. Their quivering noses betray their burrows. He looks
for ptarmigan, a small bird with brown feathers that turn
white as a wintertime disguise. He traps polar bear occasionally; mink, marten, muskrat and wolverine often. Their fur
will be sold far to the south, with some kept to line and trim
family wardrobes. Sometimes he travels on a sled he made
himself, pulled by his fat, furry, Husky dog. How does he
see in the dark? The moon and his flashlight, white beams
on the snow.

More than twenty-six hundred miles across Canada to the
southeast, Ivan Emberley lives in Rushoon, an outport on the
island of Newfoundland. Outport is the Newfoundlander's
name for a fishing village. Ivan is the same age as Rodney
and also an expert bike rider. In Rushoon, it's 4:30 A.M. when
Rodney in Tuk is biking at midnight. The night before,
Ivan had ridden through summer twilight to the fish processing plant where his mother works nights. Waiting beside a
chute outside with other boys, he watched for discarded
fish heads, cod tongues and small fish to slither down the

5

chute. He can make up to $100 a month selling these discards.

His father repairs boats. Sometimes he fishes himself and takes Ivan along. The fleet of white skiffs leaves the deep tidal inlet of Rushoon usually between two and four in the morning and returns around five-thirty in the afternoon. A phone rings in the Emberley house. Someone at the plant calls to say the fishermen have been sighted on their way to harbor. That's when his mother goes to work. If the call comes early, she may have to leave for Ivan's fifteen-year-old sister, Joanne, some task she didn't have time enough to finish. Tonight, it's feeding a baby granddaughter. Joanne takes over as soon as she slides from the oven a cake she has just baked.

Shortly Ivan and his father come home. After a damp day on the boat the birchwood fire in the kitchen stove smells and feels good. Fish run best in fog and rain, fishermen say, and Newfoundland gets plenty of both. Ivan is glad he helped his mother gather that wood. He also smells the cake and grabs a hunk, not waiting for it to cool and be frosted. Joanne rolls her eyes to the ceiling, but says nothing. She's busy feeding the baby. She is growing up to be a Newfoundland outport woman.

Like many of the Rushoon people, the Emberleys are descended from the Irish who were some of Newfoundland's first settlers. You can still hear a brush of gentle Irish brogue in the speech of these outporters.

In the middle of Canada, you can hear Icelandic. Not far from the town of Riverton, Manitoba, is a stretch of prairies that Icelanders cleared, plowed and tilled, harrowed and seeded into breadbaskets for the nation. Julianna and Valdine Bjornson live there. Great-grandfather Bjornson was

Iceland-born. Father Bjornson still speaks the language with relatives who work with him, and has taught the girls Icelandic folk songs. Their mother's parents came from Germany. Julianna, twelve, and Valdine, ten, have studied both languages in school. In their area, if twenty families request teaching in a certain language, the children receive it.

The girls' father, Bjorn—"Barney" to Canadian friends—raises some thirteen hundred acres of trefoil, wheat, lentils, or whatever crop seems wisest for the soil, the weather and the price to be had in any given year. There's a lot of two kinds of work in raising grain: guesswork and hard work.

In the busy harvest time, Valdine, Julianna and their mother take supper out to the fields. The family eats, then continues working until stopped by the dew or the dark. Even on an ordinary day, they meet in the fields for the four o'clock afternoon break of coffee and homemade cake.

Valdine and Julianna have their chores. They help preserve and freeze the fruits and vegetables the Bjornson family raises for their own use along with the cash grain crops. The girls also mow the lawn. Each one mows a third, their mother the other third. They feed the turkeys, rabbits, chickens and geese, looking anxiously for signs of the red fox that steals them. If they hear a honking in the late summer afternoons, they search the skies, hoping the migrating wild geese will find other fields to roost in for the night. The geese can strip several acres of grain for dinner.

But the girls still have time for fun. Summers, they swim in Lake Winnipeg, about four miles from their farm. Winters, they skate in their driveway. Their father turns it into a rink. In the endlessly flat prairieland he also makes hills for sliding by mounding up the heavy snows with his caterpillar tractor. Their eyes are used to the prairies' vastness, white in

7

winter, in summer a patchwork of ambers and ochres, greens and gold.

Their whole country is big—ten percent bigger than the United States and second in size only to the Soviet Union. The size makes room for differences—a bit like a circus tent covering different spectacles in different rings. Not only do Canadians come from assorted backgrounds, they are also confronted with problems and opportunities that vary with the climate and natural environment where they happen to live. And the great distances between communities make it easy for people to keep their own ways, rather than becoming Xerox copies of others.

This immense land is ribbed with mountains, crested with ice, rolled out in plains, snaked with rivers and pocked with lakes that add up to a third of the world's fresh water. It is furred with forest that supplies almost half the world's newsprint paper. Canada is rich in some of our planet's most sought-for minerals, from platinum, silver, gold and oil to copper, lead, zinc, iron, nickel and asbestos. The wheat and beef farmers raise on the Canadian plains make the country a leading exporter of these foods. The rivers supply unending power for the production of electricity, some of which is sold to the power-hungry United States. Although a majority of the almost twenty-four-and-a-half million Canadians live in the country's southeast, the west is now growing faster than the east. Its cities are sprawling farther and farther into the countryside because of the numbers of people moving westward.

East or west, much of the life-style of boys and girls takes off from what their province has and does along with ethnic customs at home. Canada is divided into ten provinces and two territories. Unlike the provinces, the territories aren't yet self-governing. The Yukon is one of them; the other is the Northwest Territories where Rodney lives. It includes the whole Canadian Arctic. Valdine's and Julianna's Manitoba is a province in the mid-section of the country. Joanne's and Ivan's home is on the island part of the province of New-foundland-Labrador on the east coast. The other provinces are Québec, Nova Scotia,, Prince Edward Island, New Brunswick in the east; Ontario, Saskatchewan, in the center; Alberta and British Columbia in the west.

British Columbia borders the Pacific Ocean. In its largest city, Vancouver, families live in apartment houses and bungalows, pressed smack up against each other. Still, every building has a tiny bit of room for the well-planted yard that's important to Canadians wherever they live. Thirteen year-old Kevin Arthur Steven Gee lives in a bungalow. His mother was born in Canton, in the People's Republic of China. His father is Canadian, born of Chinese parents.

When Kevin started school, others teased him because he had no middle name. So his parents gave him two middle names. Thereafter, he was one up on most of his classmates.

Kevin's greatest joys are figure skating and ice hockey. Mostly, girls are figure skating stars. Kevin, who is very skilled, is an exception. Exercise keeps Kevin warm in the deep cold of the ice rink, but some of his forty relatives who may come to watch shiver despite warm clothing

All the relatives are frequently in each others' homes, especially so on Chinese holidays or family birthdays. On such occasions, everybody cooks a great deal and eats a great deal—always Chinese food, always eaten with chopsticks. All observe Chinese table manners. No one lifts a chopstick before Father does. No one guzzles or bangs on the table. But everyone stuffs. The host father keeps loading the plates and it's not considered polite to leave any.

The adults often talk in Chinese at such gatherings, provided they can all speak the same dialects. The language has a good many. The children prefer English. Several of them take lessons in Chinese in special schools. They still prefer English. But they mix Chinese and Canadian ways comfortably, following the Chinese fashion at home, the Canadian fashion outside.

On some occasions, like Christmas, the two life-styles meld at home. Children look forward to traditional gift giving, stocking hanging and tree trimming. They also look forward to the big Christmas dinner. It's strictly Chinese.

Most Chinese boys and girls have as many "Occidental" as Chinese friends. "Occidental," which means western, is their name for non-Chinese. Kevin's closest pal, D.J. (short for David John) Walker, also thirteen, is an Occidental. The two practice hockey together weekends and go to hockey camp together summers. Ice hockey is as much a passion with Canadians as baseball or basketball is with Americans. Some boys start learning the sport when they are only five or six. Kevin and D.J. have a collection of hockey cards with photos of star players, which they swap, much as baseball cards are swapped in the States. Both want to be hockey pros when they grow up.

Unlike Kevin and D.J., French Canadian young people tend to choose friends among themselves. Home for most of them is Canada's biggest province and its least integrated with the others, Québec.

The Québecois are descendants of early explorers and the first European colonizers and settlers of North America, including Canada. These pioneers were French. They founded and nurtured settlements and trading posts as far west as the Mississippi River, north around Hudson's Bay, and as far south as Louisiana. Québec was their headquarters. In 1759, the English besieged, invaded and conquered Québec. Three years later, France ceded all Canada to England as part of a treaty ending a European war of which France had wearied.

The English governors who took over were sometimes understanding of their new subjects, sometimes not. The French baffled them. They simply refused to become English. To make matters worse, a few years after the English victory, Canada was flooded by English and pro-English who had fled there to escape from the American Revolution to the south. These newcomers gladly accepted English rule and had little sympathy for the French. The French Canadians felt truly deserted. The mother country had bargained them away; they had foreign rulers and were swamped by foreign refugees. On occasion, their resentment flamed into armed rebellion. Such conflicts continued, flaring up as late as the 1970s.*

Only traces remain today, however. The big change followed the Official Languages Act, which became fully effective in 1978. Briefly, this law makes both French and English official languages of Canada and contains clauses that require people who want to work in government or government-related jobs to speak both. Within Québec, French is *the* official language. A majority of French Canadians can speak English. A majority of the English can't speak French. Many are not eager to learn. The English are not happy with this law. But the French are.

---

* For the full story of the French in North America and the subsequent French plight from 1534 to the present, see *The French Founders of North America and Their Heritage*, by Sabra Holbrook, Atheneum, 1976, N.Y.

Before the language law came into being, French-speaking Canadians, who are almost a third of the population, faced all sorts of vexing and perplexing problems. In the telephone book their names were translated. Pierre became Peter; Monique, Monica. Policemen and firemen, post office clerks, judges and juries spoke only English. Trials were conducted in English.

The language law put a stop to such practices. It restored a sense of dignity to French Canadians. Most important of all, it opened doors to good jobs. If some English-speaking Canadians still call French fellow citizens "pea soupers," because they like rich pea soup, or "frogs," for French; if they still tell them to "speak white" should they slip into French, well, shrug the Québecois, let them. Talk doesn't matter so much if one's wallet is fat.

That's why the drive for Québec independence, which crested in the 1970s, attracts far fewer followers today. The Québecois are earning more and see a chance of more to come. The idea of independence, now called by a softer name, sovereignty-association, is rather like an invitation to a party pasted in a scrap book of souvenirs; preserved but yellowing.

Boys and girls in Québec know all about this struggle. They have an extra-strong sense of provincial loyalty. Thirteen-year-old France and ten-year-old Ninon Groulx will tell you that they are first Québecoise and secondly Canadian. Their fifteen-year-old, pipe-smoking brother, Fabien, doesn't claim to be either one. "*Je suis,*" he says. I am. His nickname is "Unique" because he is an only son in a family of six girls.

Fabien shares some tastes, however, with other Québecois boys and men. He loves a rocking chair. Practically every Québecois home has one, often in the big, living-room-like kitchen, where cooking, sewing, reading, game-playing may all go on at once. In the Groulx kitchen, Fabien rocks with Honoré or Balzac, the Groulx dogs, at his side, and possibly Virgule, the Groulx cat, in his lap. Honoré Balzac, whose first and last name the dogs have inherited, was a famous French novelist of the nineteenth century. Virgule is so named because he curls his tail like a comma. "Virgule" is French for comma.

All three pets hope for bits of the *pet de soeur* Fabien may munch when not puffing his pipe. Pet de soeur is a curlicue of piecrust, laden with maple syrup and baked to a golden crisp. It's very popular with Québec boys and girls. Ninon can make it. She is learning to be a good cook. France already is. Both girls help their mother with the cooking, which is all from scratch, including the daily loaves of bread. The girls' dresses are made of bright colored cotton, printed with a native Québecois print—tiny flowers. Even the smallest wear little gold rings in their pierced ears.

Their home, the Manoir de Laterriere, not far from the town of Chicoutimi, is a huge, rambling chalet, set in 200 acres of woodland. The Québec flag, a white cross on a blue field, with a white fleur-de-lis in each of the four blue corners, flies in their front yard. The fleur-de-lis was the emblem of the French when they founded Canada.

Not without reason are the Groulx acres called a *manoir*. That was the name sometimes given to large estates by early settlers. Whole families shared the responsibility of maintaining the land. Fabien helps his father take care of the forest; parents and children all work in the vegetable garden. There's a difference, though. The early settlers had tenant workers. The Groulx do it themselves. Nevertheless, when Mother

13

and Father are seated at each end of the long, Québec wood dinner table, with all the children between, the scene would fit in a movie about French pioneers.

The French are the largest, but only one of the many ethnic backgrounds that make up Canada. Icelandic, German, Eskimo, North American Indians, East Indians, Chinese, Ukrainian, Finnish, Irish, Portugese, Italians; these are some of the others. Among them, an echo is often to be heard of France and Ninon Groulx's "I am first Québecoise." Valdine and Julanna Bjornson say "I am first Icelandic-German." Sometimes it's the background, sometimes the province, which claims first allegiance. An American newspaperman, once mistaken for a Canadian by his television host, attempted to correct the error. "I'm not Canadian," he said. His host interrupted, "I'm not either. I'm a Newfoundlander." British Columbians, whose desire to run their own affairs has been second only to Québec's, often identify themselves first with their province. So do Albertans.

The fact is that every province is, in many matters, a law unto itself. Example: To get a treaty permitting Canada and the United States to dam the Columbia River together took three years because British Columbia balked. Canada's federal (national) government couldn't sign without British Columbia's agreement, because Canadian provinces have independent control over their waterways. The source of the Columbia River and much of its flow is in British Columbia. Only when the United States came up with an offer of well over 250 billion dollars, as advance payment for use of the waterpower the damned river would produce, plus money for flood control, did British Columbia give consent.

Education is another of the powers held almost completely by the provinces. How many days boys and girls go to school, what they study, when school opens and shuts, how many grades it has—all these questions are up to the provinces —and the answers are rarely the same in any two.

In a number of ways the economic life of the whole nation can be controlled by provinces. The price of oil, found abundantly in the west, especially in Alberta, is an example. Alberta took the lead in setting the price for the nation—a sky-high one. "Before we found oil, we had to beg from you," said the westerners. "Now you know what it feels like."

Recently, oil has been discovered in the Atlantic Ocean, off the coast of Newfoundland. The federal government says since the find is offshore it belongs to the nation. "No way," say the Newfoundlanders. Natural resources belong to the provinces. They intend to outdo the westerners. The debate rages on.

Meanwhile, the Emberleys in Newfoundland heat their home in winter with their wood stove, because western heating oil costs too much, despite an agreement the federal government finally reached with Alberta for somewhat lower prices.

Such problems arise from the nature of Canada's Constitution. From 1867 until 1982, the country's supreme law was the British North American Act, established by England in Canada's colonial days. The act created a very loose alliance among the provinces, a confederation, much like the alliance of the thirteen American colonies before they agreed on a constitution creating a true federation. In it, the states delegate to a central government those powers vital for the well-being of the whole nation.

For years, attempts to create a similar type of constitu-

15

tion for Canada failed, because no province was ready to delegate authority. Then—at a time of rising prices and fewer jobs—a change came. Perhaps hoping that a united government could find better remedies than any province alone, all the provinces except Québec agreed in 1981 to delegate much, though not all, of the authority they had once kept to themselves. The next year the new document was approved by the British Parliament and became—with Québec dissenting—Canada's own. "I wish simply," said the nation's Prime Minister, Pierre Trudeau, "that the bringing home of our Constitution marks the end of a long winter, the breaking up of the ice-jams and the beginning of a new spring."

The "new spring" has a catch in it, however. The catch is that any provincial legislature may pass laws contradicting the new Constitution. Such laws apply only in the provinces where they are passed and are good only for five years. Still, if a provincial legislature wants to renew such a law at that time, it can. So the provinces have the last word.

The most important addition to the Constitution is a Charter of Rights and Freedoms, something like the Bill of Rights in the United States Constitution, but with more specific concern for more people. The rights of the elderly, non-English speaking citizens and the mentally and physically handicapped are carefully spelled out. The text outlaws unfair treatment not only because of "race, national or ethnic origin, colour, religion," but also because of "sex." It provides broad protection of individual rights in very modern terms.

Adopting and abiding by a constitution are two quite different things, however. There is little unity of feeling across the country. West and East exchange insults. The English resent the French; the French have no love for the

*Grain elevators interrupt the
flat prairie skyline.*

English. Other minorities insist that if French can be an official language, theirs should be, too. Still the country is so big and its resources are so many, that Canadian families, regardless of what they call themselves and others, survive, progress in spite of hardships and preserve their chosen lifestyles.

Except for one group: the Indians.

CHAPTER **2**

Canada's Native Peoples —Indians

THE FIRST PEOPLE TO SET FOOT ON SOIL THAT BECAME CANADA were those who are today known as Indians. They came some eleven thousand years ago from a part of the world today called Siberia, in the Soviet Union. They crossed the narrow Bering Strait to the jutting shores of land that is now Alaska. Even before the glaciers of the ice age had fully disappeared, they hunted out ice-free corridors along the mountains, eventually gaining interior valleys. With good reason do Indians of Canada consider white people, with a history of less than 500 years, as newcomers. More, they are apt to consider them thieves. From the Indian point of view, white people stole their wilderness.

Canada's quarter million Indians live mostly in the northern part of the country—a majority in the northwest. The bands have tribal names; among main ones, the Chipewa,

*The Indian boys' "wide game"
upsets the girls' washline*

Yellowknife, Dogrib, Hare, Nahanni, Slave, Micmac, and Kutchin.

Kutchin, means, simply, the people. So does Dene, a general name, preferred to "Indian," by many of those living in the mid-north and northeast. Eleven-year-old Keith Kunnizi is a Kutchin. He lives in Fort McPherson, a village in the Northwest Territories. The village is not all Indian. There are only a few all-Indian villages or reserves in Canada, though Indians and other Canadians usually separate into different sections of a town.

Keith and his two younger sisters live with their mother, their grandparents and an uncle. Keith has no idea who his father was. He's never seen him. His mother cooks in Fort McPherson's motel, except for now and then, when she has drunk too much to go to work.

One Christmas she bought Keith a guitar, for which she had saved a long while. Keith, who has a quick ear for music, picked out tunes for himself. His friends sang along with him. Where Keith went, his guitar went and there was song. He and his guitar seemed like one person who was able to make everybody feel better.

Well, not everybody. One winter night his uncle staggered home with a friend. Both men had been drinking too much. The friend didn't like Keith's music. He lunged at him, fists clenched. Keith raised the guitar across his face to protect himself. The man grabbed the guitar and smashed it against the wall. Keith ran outside into the snow.

His mother began saving up again. Next Christmas there was another guitar for Keith. A new teacher in school started showing Keith how to read music so he needn't rely only on his ear. With his new knowledge he can also strum tunes he's never heard. But now Keith is wary where he plays. He is afraid of another smashup.

One memorable summertime, Keith camped with other young Indians from the Northwest and Yukon Territories at Moosehide, on a bluff above the Yukon River. The campsite was once a stopover for free-roaming Indians who followed the trails of caribou. A few log cabins, lop-sided with age and weather, lean on the site, but now most people bring their own tents. Once arrived, they cut birch poles for tent ridges and supports. They gather firewood for cooking. At mealtime, there's never any need to call boys and girls to the open air benches and tables. The rich scent of salmon, fresh-caught from the river below, mingled with wood smoke, is signal enough. Trouble is, Indian manners require that the elders be served first!

The campers come from long distances. Often their buses are shaky, the windows and windshields pocked by sharp gravel flying up from the roads, the tires worn thin and smooth. Five or six flat tires along the way aren't uncommon. The passengers are patient. The prospect ahead is where their thoughts are.

At Dawson City, in the Yukon, people and tents, cartons of food, cooking utensils and washtubs are transferred from the buses to flat-bottomed boats with outboard motors. Knowledgeable pilots zigzag the craft along the river, ducking adverse currents, taking advantage of those flowing their way. At the foot of the bluff where the camp is perched, the boats are unloaded. Everything is lugged to the top.

Once settled in, campers follow a daily round of something for everyone and everyone for something. There are religious services, language courses, lectures, turns to be taken at cooking and cleaning up. Elders may choose to sit around the campfire and talk about when they were young.

There's storytelling by night and games by day. Most of the games are called "wide games," meaning players can run and roam at will, hemmed in by no boundaries. In the flag game, three or more teams compete. Each member makes a flag from a rag or discarded plastic bag attached to a stick. His aim is to capture the flags of opponents. When a flag bearer is caught, he tries to hurl his emblem to a member of his own team. It may be intercepted in midair, of course. The air soon becomes full of sticks and bags and rags. The winning team is the one that captures them all.

Horseback is another wide game. Two teams stand face to face, half of each team mounted on the shoulders of the other half. The object is to knock the riders off the backs of their "horses." The winner is the team with one or more riders still seated.

In the course of such games players run up and down hill, through meadow and woodland, with no restrictions, as once their ancestors roamed the North American continent. The entire camp program is meant to help today's Indians refeel the Indian spirit of long ago. They learn what it's like to travel on the river, live from the land and water. For certain, children of the early Indians didn't snack on peanut butter and jelly sandwiches as these young people do; nevertheless, the camp gets across to them that they come from a rich background, the gift of a generous earth.

Courses in Kutchin are one of the ways they sample their past. They discover the names of familiar animals: the grizzly bear—*shih*, rabbit—*geh*; muskrat—*dzan*. The trap for snaring such animals is a *kyah*. They learn to call their caribou hide boots *kaitrih*. They master the Kutchin alphabet, which has combinations of sounds entirely new to them, like ddh as in *ddhan*, mountain, or dl, as in *dlak*, squirrel. The language course is like another game. It rouses a lot of enthusiasm. And perhaps being able to speak some Kutchin also makes them proud. Only Kutchins can talk like that.

These young people need pride. Their families have lost the old Indian ways, the ways of the wanderer, following caribou trails, hunting, fishing, living close to and respecting the land, respecting their elders, tending and tender with their young. Nor have they yet replaced their old ways with the new life-styles of white men who took over their lands. Hordes of them have swarmed in, once digging for gold, now for oil; once exploring land, now denuding it for countless other riches. The white man bulldozes into motel-dotted roads the trails that connected Indian hunting grounds; he dams their salmon rivers for water power. He turns their campsites into mining towns. In these towns conveniences are many. Stoves, refrigerators, plumbing, supermarkets. And bars and liquor stores.

Not yet part of this new way of living, admiring its conveniences, which are costly, the Canadian Indian is untrained in how to produce them. With a lost past and a frustrating present, he is betwixt and between. He is in limbo. So he goes to the bar or the liquor store. They are his escape from his nowhere.

Alcoholism is a family problem that injures many young Indians like Keith Kunnizi. He stands to lose more than his guitar. If Keith follows the general pattern of today, he will, in just a few more years, inherit responsibility for the family. He will drop out of school and go to work at whatever job an untrained boy can find.

Family responsibility falls first on the shoulders of the oldest boy or girl. The father may have disappeared, as in Keith's case, or he may be too done in by drinking to work. Mother usually becomes the wage earner when father quits. In time, she too begins to seek comfort in alcohol. That's when the oldest child becomes mother and father. When the same thing happens to him, the next oldest takes over.

Some agencies, public and private, are trying to help Canada's Indians climb out of their limbo. By far the most widespread and sensitive efforts are those of the Anglican and Roman Catholic Churches. Theirs is a real crusade. But Keith and his friends will need even more help if they are to find meaning in life.

Part of the Moosehide camping program is a series of talks for campers by Indians who have beaten the alcohol problem. Their advice: "Don't take the first drink. Don't let friends call you chicken if you don't. They are the chickens. You stick with your tea." Indian boys and girls are very fond of tea. They drink quantities of it. They listen to some of the talks, but not all. They aren't accustomed to paying attention very long. Besides, they are eager to return to their games and their gold panning.

In 1898, the Yukon was the scene of a great gold rush. Some one hundred thousand people, dreaming of fortunes, ravaged cliffs and rivers. They made off with almost all the bounty. But because the price of gold has skyrocketed today, a new generation of fortune seekers has arrived with modern equipment in an attempt to find what little may be left. The young Indians, trying to sift gold from a frothing stream, don't find anything except shiny mica. Never mind. It's fun to splash in the swift running current.

Even in the rain, the campers play outdoors. Their

25

clothes become sodden, but nobody complains. A plastic cover, suspended on hastily cut birch trunks, protects the fire and the dining area. At night, the children gather round the fire for stories. Some are modern ghost thrillers. Some are old Indian myths. There may be a cup of hot moose soup before a late bedtime in a leaky tent.

The rain is better than the blizzards of winter and the cold that frosts Keith's eyeglasses. Going to school, he ties a scarf over his face and is careful not to breathe too deeply. If he does, the cold will burn his lungs. The tires on his school bus freeze into squares. The driver starts the blanketed engine and leaves it running. Gradually the tires round out again. In the Canadian north, little more than is absolutely necessary goes on outdoors in winter. Rain or shine, young people make the most of the brief summer.

As twelve-year-old Ruby Lucille Vanettsi, another Moose-hide camper, puts it: "Do it get cold up here. I so hurry for the summer. Then I sit out at a hill and draw beautiful trees and water." Ruby is tall and slender, with shoulder-length, straight black hair, long-lashed brown eyes and full lips. Other campers like to watch her sketch the river and its wooded banks.

What will become of Keith and his music, Ruby and her art? By law, they should finish high school. They are fortunate in having one in their town. But their future will depend on family circumstances more than on law.

Says Mrs. Dora Robinson: "The family has fallen apart." Mrs. Robinson, an Indian, is the Social Assistance Administrator for Indian families in Kitimat, British Columbia. The Indian section of the town, spelled *Kitimaat* in the local Indian dialect, is one of few places where some bits of the old Indian culture live on. Some of the last totem poles to be found in all Canada (except for mock images set up for tourists outside supermarkets and tourist information points) stand in Kitimaat. A totem pole tells in carvings the history of a clan, which is a subdivision of a tribe. The clans of Kitimaat are the Eagles, the Ravens, the Beavers, the Killer Whales and the Fish. Each has its own chief and council of elders.

The trouble is that now these traditional leaders have no power. "The government tells us," says Mrs. Robinson, "that only the people elected by their ballots can make laws. So our leaders have lost respect.

"Our people don't understand the way white government works. Our leaders have to be above wrongdoing. Theirs don't. Their workers don't meet us directly. If a child isn't working well in school, or is sick, the teacher tells the public health nurse, who tells me, and I tell the parent. The parents get mad at this. If an Indian finds a child in trouble, he takes him home to his parents.

"Teachers tell children: 'Send your mother in.' Mothers don't go. They expect the teacher to come to them, as any Indian would do. Then the teacher asks the child: 'Where's your mother?' The child doesn't know what to say, so he doesn't answer. The teacher thinks he's dumb. It's always the child who suffers.

"After school, he has little to do. Once boys helped fathers build canoes. Girls helped mothers grow and prepare food. Now the parents buy things instead of make them. And what they can afford to buy isn't very good. So neither is the children's health."

Some Indians have banded together in organizations such as COPE, the Indian Brotherhood of the Northwest Territories, and the Council of Yukon Indians, in an effort to change this picture. Their common goal is to regain the lands their ancestors once owned. Others are trying to work through white government. In the Northwest Territories, a team-up with Eskimos has succeeded in electing a majority of these groups to the Council that advises the Territories' federal commissioner.

Self-help projects, matching old skills to new opportunities, also bring hope. One such project is the fish processing plant near Dawson in the Yukon. Saint Paul's Anglican Church, the founder of Moosehide Camp, is also the founder of the plant. Fishing skills have been important to Indians for centuries. The Dawson fish processing plant is sometimes so laden with salmon that the young Deacon of Saint Paul's has to rush all over town finding freezer space for the overload. If the plant freezer breaks down, the problem is worse still. The fishermen keep coming, but it may be days before a repairman can make his way up from Vancouver. You can smell salmon all over the town of Dawson when that happens.

Fogo Island, a jagged rock of an island near the Atlantic coast of Newfoundland, is also Indian territory. Spurred by the Memorial University of Newfoundland's field service, several agencies have helped the islanders set up a fish processing cooperative in which all fishermen own shares.

The co-op has made a tremendous difference in their lives. Once children could attend school in the short summer only, because no teacher would brave the desolate winters with ramshackle housing and pittance pay. The children's clothing was patched rags. Though fish was plenteous, the only method of preserving it was drying in the sun. The only method of transportation was horse-drawn carts. Logs, for building and heating, were generally lugged on homemade stretchers from the interior forest.

An Indian village, Queen Charlotte Islands, British Columbia.

By no means can Fogo today be called prosperous. But the improvements are heartening. There's money for winter school, for children's clothing, for trucks and tractors. The money comes from fish properly prepared for waiting markets in a processing plant that also pays good wages to workers.

In films of the old Fogo, children are a sad-looking lot. Today, as they plây their island games, they grin and shout. They are clever at making toys, stilts, boats, rafts. They guide their boats by tying them to sticks with long strings. Tin cans are ballast. Toy boat races are great weekend fun. So are stilt races and raft sailing. The rafts are made from forest logs, the sails from potato sacks.

The boys are lively jig dancers. The jig came to Newfoundland with the early Irish settlers. The foot-stomping rhythm appealed to the Indians. Fogo boys will dance it anywhere their boots can make enough clop-clop. Usually, they are accompanied by a harmonica player, who sharply accents his tunes. If one boy starts a jig, another and another are sure to join in.

Canada's young Indians need more of what is happening to them and their families in Fogo and Dawson and at Moosehide. Descendants of the first people to live with the country's wilderness, they have what it takes to join those who—with the aid of modern equipment—are putting natural resources to work on wide scales. Indians, too, need to be discovered.

CHAPTER 3

Canada's Native Peoples
–Eskimos

LIKE CANADA'S INDIANS, THE ESKIMOS ORIGINALLY CROSSED THE Bering Strait from Asia. They came later than the Indians— about six thousand years ago—and there are fewer of them today, only twenty thousand. They don't have tribes, but their groups are divided by dialects: the Copper, the Mackenzie, more often called Alaskan, the Caribou and the Baffin. Actually, though the groups remain distinct and live mostly in their own communities, the dialects are less and less spoken, except by older people. Boys and girls speak English. Some, mainly in the midnorth and northeast, call themselves Inuit. Like the Indian word "Dene," Inuit means "the people."

Rodney Raddi and his friends in the Arctic village of Tuk are Alaskan Eskimos. Although their ancestors were wanderers, they now lead settled lives. They have fewer problems than Indians in combining old and new ways. With

*Eskimo children of Inuvik
swinging outside school.*

fewer problems, there's less seeking escape in liquor. However, Eskimos may ban its sale in a community where they foresee danger.

One reason Eskimos adapt with less trouble to new ways may be their fewer numbers. Another is certainly their staunch independence. The Canadian Eskimo chooses which of his own ways he wants to keep and he keeps them, no matter what. He is unstoppable in his choices. He also chooses which of the white man's ways he wants to adopt. He manages the two together like a man who has hitched up two horses to his cart.

During the annual spring camp-out, the way is all Eskimo. Rodney and his family and the whole village of Tuk take off. The flat spit of land the village occupies, reaching out into the Arctic Ocean's Beaufort Sea, is deserted. School closes: there aren't any pupils. They are traveling in Ski-Doos with their parents to the Husky Lakes, the traditional hunting grounds for Tuk Eskimos. Rodney and his friends call lakes ponds. Far north lakes are indeed pond-sized puddles. They lie close together, hundreds upon hundreds of them, stretching over miles and miles. In summer they dot the Arctic with brown water muddied by the melted top layer of permafrost.

Eskimos camp while the pond ice is solid. They pitch sturdy canvas tents—igloos have long since been forsaken—and ready their guns for shooting game. At ten, Rodney has his own gun. He handles it with ease because his father started teaching him how when he was five.

The camp is a hubbub of activity. Rodney's sisters and mother skin the furs from animals he and his father shoot or trap. The womenfolk also smoke the fish men catch from under the ice. The aroma of fish smoking above a low fire is

33

so tempting, and the golden color so inviting, that boys and girls tear off tastes even before the smoking is finished.

Between chores, Rodney races his husky dog with others. Huskies are no longer used for transportation. The Ski-Doos have replaced the dog. But they are very much in evidence as family pets. They also make fine racers and good animals for pulling young people's sleds.

The people of Tuk will stay in camp until the ice, beginning to break up, threatens a safe homeward passage for the Ski-Doos. Their departure depends on nature. Eskimo time is a matter of season, or else when people are ready, rather than clocks or calendars. A school teacher who is a "southerner"—the Eskimo way of describing white people—has a hard time understanding this habit at first. Their pupils are often late for school. School has to wait until they arrive.

Parents don't push children to be what southerners call "on time." In fact, parents frequently let them follow their own wishes, unless they try something that could be dangerous. Then they are punished—but almost never with a slap or a spanking. To hurt a child physically is unthinkable to most Eskimo mothers and fathers. The children, in turn, have great respect for their parents. They are likely to do what they are told.

The family is close. Everybody shares work and fun. Rodney and other boys may mop floors or wash dishes right along with their sisters. The oldest, whether boy or girl, helps take care of younger ones. In the cold of sunless, deep winter, the family lives mostly inside. Outdoors, the ice is too thick even to stretch nets under it for herring. Blizzards blow. Snow mounts in twenty-foot drifts. The temperature drops to fifty-eight degrees below Fahrenheit (— fifty degrees Celsius). The town is still, the streets deserted.

Indoors, life is active. Parents and older boys and girls carve from whalebone, caribou antlers and soapstone little figures of Eskimos and animals, which sell for high prices in southern Canadian cities. New clothing is fashioned and old clothing repaired. Parkas, some jacket length, some down to the ankles, are stitched from caribou hide, lavishly embroidered with beads. The hoods are lined with mink, wolverine, or other fur. Because the fur frames the face like rays, these hoods are called sunbursts.

Some of the parkas are made for baby-carrying. These are extra-large. The baby is belted in on the mother's back, its head sharing the mother's sunburst. The custom is known as "packing a baby." In the northeast, the baby-packing parka is called an *amawt*. Little girls play dress-up games in them. The amawt, or baby-packing parka, is the reason for backless pews in far north churches with Eskimo congregations. Babies would be squashed by a pew back.

Winter also offers a breather for *mukluk* making. Mukluks are velvet-soft, caribou hide boots, embroidered at the top. The soles are moosehide or sealskin. Inside these, people wear another pair, made of wool, called duffles. As all this work goes on—so does the TV. In January and February, the deepest winter months, it's stitch and watch, watch and stitch.

More and more mothers balance outside jobs with running homes. Some are airline stewardesses. Others teach, or work in hospitals, offices, stores, motels. Eskimo men are in demand on oil riggers or pipe lines. They are employed in mines, as mechanics, heavy machinery operators and carpenters. They have a reputation for willingness to work hard and well. All across the Arctic both men and women may help operate the DEW Line. DEW stands for distant early warning. This joint Canadian-United States operation can warn of enemy attack launched from far-off skies.

Some Eskimos run their own businesses. The Mayor of Tuk, for example, does well with his large reindeer herd. These animals, valuable for both meat and hide, are born to be wanderers, foragers for their food: grass and lichens, a form of moss.

Keeping reindeer in one place requires a lot of land and a lot of fencing. Fortunately, there's plenty of vacant land in the Arctic. The fencing, with permafrost and snowdrifts, is more of a problem. Rounding up the animals in winter is a problem, too. Their tan coats whiten like the snow-covered ground, so that they are hard to spot. Close enough up, however, they can be heard pawing. Their hooves turn concave in winter, not only giving them a good grip on ice and snow, but allowing them to dig through it for lichens.

A reinder herder must keep constant track of his charges. Bears and wolves try to keep track of them, too! Raising reindeer requires a twenty-four hour alert. Frequently, Mayor Nasogaluak helicopters out to his range to make sure the herders living there have everything under control.

When the Mayor wants to inspect his reindeer herd, that's what he does. When it's camp time, everybody camps. When, in summer, the beluga whales come through, seekers of *ok-shok*, whale oil, or *muck-tuk*, blubber, or whale meat, are off for twenty-four hours in huge canoes. Sometimes they are off longer, camping on an island, waiting for the whales. When snow melts from the ice, and ice softens, tea lovers paddle out to collect the slush. They say it makes the best water for brewing tea. Businesses run by southerners who employ Eskimos have to manage schedules on Eskimo time. That's the way of the Arctic.

Southerners, as well as Eskimos and Indians, look forward to the Northern Games, an Eskimo springtime festival, held each year in a different part of the Northwest Territories. The games are contests in which Eskimos show off their special arts and skills. There are harpoon hurling, seal skinning and bannock baking contests. Bannock is a rich, fried dough. Canoes are raced; paintings, carvings and embroidery are displayed. Blanket tossing, like jumping on a trampoline, is a popular attraction. The winner is the one who stays on his feet longest. In the past, Eskimos stretched walrus skins for this competition, but these days walrus is too precious for such frivolity.

Paintings by Eskimo boys and girls, usually of flowers, boats and animals, win a lot of ribbons. Many Eskimo young people are skilled at capturing their natural surroundings on paper, cloth, canvas, even burlap bags—whatever's available. They are also strong, well-coordinated athletes. Crowds give them rousing cheers for running and jumping. And crowds there are. Mothers, fathers, children, grandparents, uncles and aunts and cousins arrive with their tents by the pick-up truck load. The merrymaking continues for three or four days before weary but satisfied participants and onlookers pack up for home.

The Northern Games usually follow close on the heels of spring camping, right after the ice breakup. And soon after, it's berry picking time. All Canada is juicy with varieties of berries, but the Arctic especially so. There are Arctic cranberries, which grow on low bushes, not in bogs; crowberries, something like a small cherry, yellowberries, blueberries and more. Since most ripen in the late summer, snow catches them before every bush can be picked clean. All the better. The snow makes a natural deep-freeze. Boys and girls and their families go out to gather the fresh-frozen leftovers in the spring.

With most young people, nature's bounties—berries, fish, caribou and moose—are favorite foods. But with the opening of supermarkets new tastes prove tempting. Junk food has reached the Arctic. Soda pop, potato chips, candy and canned foods are taking a toll in skin and teeth troubles. Since fresh vegetables are hard to come by in the short Arctic growing season and imported ones are very expensive, far north peoples are especially subject to diseases that come from the lack of vegetable vitamins and minerals. Substituting store foods for food they catch or pick makes this tendency worse. The southerners' imports are threatening Eskimos' health and their appearance.

Their normal appearance is handsome. When Rodney and his sisters dress for church, they are a smart picture. In summer, Rodney wears crisp jeans and a sport shirt, maybe with a jacket. His sisters dress in flowered and ruffled muu-muus. In winter, boys and girls put on their richly embroidered, furred parkas; jacket length over pants for boys, ankle-length parkas for girls. Both boys and girls like bangs. Boys favor Dutch cuts, parted in the middle and swept to each side. Girls prefer long hair, sometimes braided, sometimes loose. Their hair is blue-black, straight and shiny. Summer weekdays, little girls often wear leotards; their older sisters wear jeans like their brothers.

Rodney's church in Tuk, Saint John's Mission, is a log cabin. On one side, near the altar, is an oil drum, which serves as a wood stove for winter heating. On the opposite side is a can of insect repellent, heavily used in early summer when biting flies and gnats can sometimes be thick enough to darken the air. The church offering plate is a furry caribou hoof, trimmed at the top with wolverine.

After church, boys and girls may ride their bikes while their parents take one of the town taxis to visit friends. A few families in Tuk have pick-up trucks, but there are no cars. People in a taxi tell the driver, "Joe's place, please," or "Cindy's," or whosoever's. There aren't any street addresses and nobody needs them, since everybody knows where everybody lives.

Sundays, or any holidays, boys may get together with their groups. Eskimo boys tend to form groups, maybe as small as six, maybe as big as sixteen. They may call the group by the number of its members: Group Six, Group Seven, and so on. Members choose their leader and make membership cards from local materials. The groups don't fight—they aren't enemies. They have no special programs. They simply play together in preference to playing with other groups.

A favorite game among all of them is *nuglugaktuk*. Each player has a long whip with which he tries to drive a ball. The ball is made of caribou hide, stuffed with lichens. Like many Eskimo games, nuglugaktuk has no rules, except that one mustn't touch the ball with hands or feet. There are no boundaries, no goals, no teams. To drive the ball is enough. A skilled player can whip it into incredible distances. The rest must then chase after it.

When high school years arrive, these groups of boys, and their sisters, too, have to leave home, if they want to go on learning. Rodney and his friends from Tuk may travel south to a boarding school in Fort McPherson or, if they are lucky, attend a modern school in Inuvik.

Inuvik, 125 miles (about 118 kilometers) south of Tuk,

39

is a thriving community of some three thousand or more Indians, Eskimos and Southerners. The cloth on the altar of the Anglican Church of the Ascension tells you something important about the two. Embroidered by a parishioner, it reads from left to right:

Rysotitinyoo Rysotitinyoo Holy Holy Nagokoyuk Nagokoyuk. The first two words are Kutchin. The third two are Alaskan Eskimo. Kutchins, Southerners and Eskimos each make up a third of Inuvik's population, an assortment of Arctic people as equally proportioned as the altar cloth.

Kirk Buckle, thirteen, son of the busy Anglican priest, is white. His best friend, John Crawford, also thirteen, is Kutchin. They fish and trap together, hunt ptarmigan and snare rabbits for the family supper. John can go after whatever prey he pleases, but not Kirk. Both Indians and Eskimos are permitted to take what they can whenever they can, without licenses, except for rod and reel fishing and in certain preserves. Southerners must be licensed. Their licenses are good only for certain seasons of the year, to protect Arctic species. In many instances, the government lacks sufficient understanding of native citizens. But when food gathering is the issue, the government is sympathetic. The laws acknowledge that for Indians and Eskimos, freedom to forage is no sport. It's a necessity.

John shares what he can spare with Kirk. Kirk in turn helps John keep his bike in good condition and train for the town bike rodeos. Both boys are bike enthusiasts. Kirk wears a pin won for a seventy-foot run, at the end of which he had to brake. Both boys join all kinds of contests for riding skills, among them, executing figure eights in and out of a course marked by pop cans, pedaling four abreast three feet apart and turning around in this formation without bumping each other. Pupils receive certificates for successful completion of bike safety and bike care courses.

Established by the government only in the last quarter century, the town of Inuvik, thanks to young, local officials and citizens who care, goes all out for its boys and girls. A popular gathering place for them is the Ingamo Recreation Hall of Friendship Center. John and Kirk often go there after school. So do Charlene and Eddie Kaglik, who are Eskimos. Charlene is ten; Eddie is twelve.

Eddie excels at scatterball, one of the indoor games frequently played at the center in winter or bad weather. The aim of the game is to hit another player with the ball. Then that player is out. The boy or girl who remains unhit, surviving alone, is the winner. Eddie's aim is accurate, his feet are nimble. He almost always wins.

His sister, Charlene, swims like a champ. In summertime, the Ingamo counselors take the children to nearby Boot Lake. The excursions are mostly on foot, about an hour's hike, or by bike. The water is so cold that youngsters duck in, splash hard and run out, putting clothes back on over their swim suits for warmth. Then, after a few moments' exercise on the sloping banks—off with jeans and T-shirts and into the lake again. And again and again and again. Charlene can stay in longer than most of the others. A counselor taught her to do the crawl. Face down, she streaks rapidly out to a small raft, hangs on to catch her breath, legs still kicking to keep warm, then streaks back in again. If the minnows are schooling, she and her friends will gather handfuls from the water and munch them raw.

Sometimes a pick-up trucker will carry boys and girls to the lake. They stand in the rear load section, waving and calling greetings to everybody on the way. Boot Lake is a favorite outing and a truck ride makes it super. At home, at the end of the day, some good hot caribou soup sends them more willingly than usual to bed No TV that night. Their eyes won't stay open any longer.

Home for Eddie and Charlene and four younger sisters and brothers is small for the family size. The once bright yellow paint is faded and peeling; the roof needs repair. One door swings loose on its hinges and the windows aren't tight. The chidren don't seem to notice. They are clothed like all their friends. They have the same T-shirts with pictures of polar bears, caribou and Eskimos throwing harpoons, which are high youth fashion in Inuvik. They attend good schools and they have plenty to eat.

Their father works as an auto mechanic; their mother has a job in the town motel. Eddie and his father trap marten, lynx and mink, which brings in extra money. There's enough for all the necessities except housing. They are on a waiting list for a housing project, but the list is long.

If their parents worked for the government instead of private business, they would live in one of the rows of vivid yellow, orange, turquoise or hot pink homes with decks around the outside, and small yards, fenced with white pickets, which fill the opposite end of town.

Little plastic greenhouses poke up from the yards, so families can grow fresh vegetables during the short summer season. Their heating, water and sewage systems are specially designed to beat the permafrost. Heat and water come in, and sewage goes out in separate above-ground pipes all enclosed in metal tubes called utiladors. They're so big around, a small child could stand upright in them. The incoming heat keeps water and sewage from freezing. The only problem is, it also keeps the water permanently hot.

*An Eskimo church
in the Arctic.*

Want a drink of cold water? Not from the faucet. Both faucets run hot. Water must be chilled in the refrigerator.

These homes have every modern convenience any family could ever want. One of the most important is a clothes dryer. For nine or ten months out of the year, clothes on an outdoor line would freeze. The rest of the time, they would be grayed with dust from the gravel roads. Only the main street is paved, and that paving was laid in such a hurry before the visit of a high government official that the material wouldn't harden properly. Charlene lost a shoe in it trying to cross!

Fathers of families in government homes are mostly highly skilled technicians, engineers and scientists, employed in exploring petrochemical possibilities. They are Southerners. The separation from the Indian and Eskimo families, at the other end of town, is not of their doing. A great many Southern parents aren't pleased with the government's housing divisions and are glad that boys and girls from the two ends of town make friends. The young Eskimos who travel from farther north to finish school in Inuvik will arrive in perhaps the most neighborly place of all for growing up in the Arctic.

CHAPTER **4**

Growing Up
in the Wilderness

TODAY ALL KINDS OF ENGINEERS ARE ON THE MOVE ACROSS Canada. They are pinpointing and developing the mineral and energy supplies that are the musts of modern civilization.

Their families travel with them, making homes in communities built from scratch. Part of a mountain may have to be bulldozed down, part of a river diverted to make room for houses, schools, churches, grocery stores, playgrounds and recreation centers. The finished product is a toy-sized town in the middle of nowhere.

Fermont is one such, located in the east in the French-speaking part of Labrador. Four-fifths of Labrador is governed by French Canadian Québec. The remaining fifth, on the Atlantic coast, is governed by Newfoundland. A bitter and stubborn dispute over this division has been going on for more than seventy years.

The people of Fermont disregard the quarrel. They are

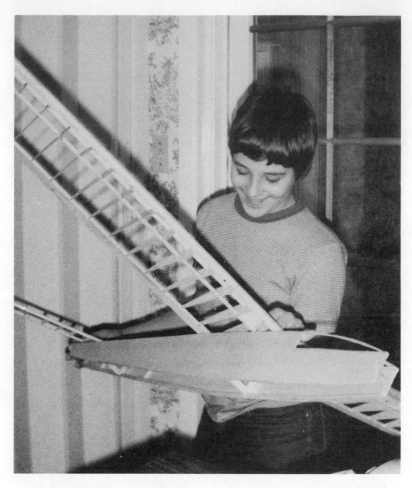

*Pierre Lanctôt and the model
plane he is making.*

there because of iron. There's a mountainful of that metal nearby. Québec-Cartier Mining, which is digging it out, at first sheltered workers and their families in trailers, but by the mid-seventies, solid housing was ready.

The village rises on an isolated plateau, surrounded by winding rivers, broad lakes and épinette-mantled mountains. The épinette is a dwarf pine, shaped like a spindle. Fermont, on the 52nd parallel, is too far north for tall vegetation. The landscape is rock and tundra: high plains of moss and low shrubs. The homes and apartment houses are built with vertical planks of red Columbian pine, which well withstands the blasts of winter.

Ten-year-old Josée Lanctôt and her twelve-year-old brother live in one of the apartment houses that wall the village from prevailing winds. Their father is the school principal. He has one thousand students in his care. If Josée and Pierre lived in a big city they couldn't find a school with better equipment or a friendlier atmosphere.

The floors are burnished ceramic tile. Every classroom has a screen for showing films or film strips. The rooms shine with color. Doors are blue, walls a sunny yellow or warm cream. Cream-colored desks have orange chairs. The semicircle of upholstered seats in the huge auditorium, rising from front to rear, faces a theater-sized stage. Theater-study groups use it constantly.

Labs and studios offer a something-for-everyone assortment of after-school activities: music, photography, yoga, painting, leatherwork, stamp collecting, macrame, nature study, Ping-Pong, radio production, school newspaper editing.

From the school library, decorated with posters showing scenes from countries around the world, students borrow an average of three to four books apiece, each week. There are three gyms for athletes, besides the outdoor hockey and soccer grounds and badminton courts.

The true life of the school, however, is more than equipment. Rather, its roots are nourished by the friendly relationship between teachers and pupils. Informality is the keynote. Boys and girls call teachers, even the principal, by first names. Teachers' names, posted on classroom doors, read "Madeleine M.," "Marie S.," and so on. Most of the teachers are wives of miners. Since everybody knows everybody, in and out of school, last names would sound silly.

Like many of the schools in Québec, school opening in the fall is called the *rentrée*, French for reentering. The rentrée resembles a huge party. Music is piped through the loudspeaker system. Color slides of school activities are shown. Quantities of fruit juice and cookies for students, coffee for their parents are served continuously from long tables. Every student is handed a welcome button. Each receives a folder, stamped with his name and classroom, containing his program and the school rules. One rule is no snowball throwing on school grounds. Snowball fights have been known to put out eyes.

The rentrée folders were assembled the day before by students themselves. Throughout the year, they often earn pocket money by helping teachers with paperwork and other chores. Staff and students make a good team. At the disco dance, when registration is over, teachers join students, not as chaperones, but as partners on the floor.

The dance is held in the *carrefour*, a French word for crossroads. In a school, it's a huge area, usually decorated with student art, from which corridors lead out to various sections of the building. The carrefour is always where the action is. At Christmas, clowns celebrate the season in the carrefour at Fermont. On such occasions, the student-run refreshment stand does a brisk business. Pierre Lanctôt is one of the stand's best customers. He and his sister are both hearty eaters. They especially like fresh-caught foods. Pierre is a good shot and expert with a rod and reel. He shoots partridge and hare with his father and fishes with him in nearby lakes and rivers. Josée is fast becoming a good fisherwoman. They like helping to bring home main dishes for supper. They also like company. When there's company for supper, they are allowed to drink a little wine, along with the grown-ups.

Their apartment makes a home that is both cozy and attractive. The furniture is carved from the blond pine of Québec forests, the walls hung with paintings by Québec artists. In the entranceway is a small organ, which both children play. In the living room is the rocking chair, so much favored by Québecois. When Pierre and Josée were a couple of years younger, they used to pile into it on top of their father, first Pierre on his lap, then Josée on Pierre's.

They didn't always live in Fermont. They were born in Montréal, the largest city in Québec, moved out to a small town, and finally still farther out to the wilderness. Their before-places are forgotten. Wilderness children live where they are, not where they came from. Many don't even identify past homes by towns. Instead, they will tell you, I came from such and such a dam, or such and such a mine. They always promise to write friends when they move, but they are soon too busy with new friends to keep their promises. Josée and Pierre knew all the children of Fermont within a week after their arrival.

Their dog is the only creature they miss. Fermont rules don't permit dogs in apartments. Children who live in the houses sheltered by the wall of apartments can have all the pets they want—and they do. Josée and Pierre are a bit jealous of them.

The houses are mostly two-family homes. Each has a garage, with doors painted in bright yellow, blue, pink or red. Many have canoes mounted on the roofs, for use in the surrounding lakes. Camper-trucks are parked in some of the yards. In summertime, children's swings are set out and lawns sprout with miniature windmills and other decorations. In winter, smoke ascends from the fireplaces where crackling logs make a cheerful sight and sound.

But winter exacts a toll from children in these houses. In thirty-five degrees below Fahrenheit (— thirty-seven degrees Celsius) temperature, they must brave whistling winds and whirling snow to reach school. They are almost hidden in their woolen face masks and heavy clothing. They look like automated bundles trudging single file.

Pierre and Josée don't so much as have to don a mitten to reach school. Apartment dwellers merely walk through a long, above-ground, heated tunnel. This same tunnel connects apartments with each other, so neighbors can visit back and forth without going outside. It leads to community facilities: a heated swimming pool, reserved at special hours for boys and girls, a grocery store, restaurant, snack bar, movie theater, stores selling drugs, hardware and clothing, and a post office for when mail comes, a newspaper stand for when newspapers arrive. Deliveries can be delayed for weeks. Pierre's twelfth birthday present from his grandparents finally reached him when he was twelve years and three months old. People learn patience in the wilderness.

50

Their patience is recompensed by "hardship pay," extra dollars to help cover high costs of food and clothing, all of which must be transported by rail and truck. Families spend some of this money on personalizing their homes. Since the layout is the same all over town, the only way to make one home different from another is to decorate it differently. Baskets of hanging plants, tanks of tropical fish, cages of bright-feathered parrots, hand-woven wall hangings, bearskin rugs, wooden carvings, beaded curtains, metalwork liven the nooks and spaces made by clever furniture arrangements. Much of the artwork is homemade. It always includes the children's drawings.

Young people are never left out of whatever is going on. They and their friends, and their parents and their parents' friends ski, hunt, fish and snowshoe together. They party together. There's just one occasion that belongs to boys and girls alone. That's the annual springtime trip to Québec City. For five days, Fermont children live in Québec homes, attending school with the young people of their host families. Then the young Québecois spend five days in Fermont. For both groups, the experience is like traveling to another world.

For Fermont boys and girls, it's a most important one. If a time comes when they must return to the city living they have forgotten, or never knew, they will already have some first-hand knowledge of what a city is like. They won't have to be scared of the unknown.

Boys and girls who grow up in the wilderness without live-in city experiences are often frightened by the idea of leaving their way of life. Thirteen year old Nancy Stone, who has grown up in Kemano, in the wilderness of British Columbia, Canada's westernmost province is facing this problem. Kemano has no high school. So Nancy is scheduled to go to school in the very pleasant city of Victoria, where she has relatives. But Nancy is sure Victoria—no matter how pleasant —can't compare with Kemano.

In Kemano she is friends with sea lions, frogs and geese as well as people. She doesn't see movies, because there's no theater. But she enjoys the nightly performance of the grizzly bears. In early evening, dozens of them muzzle and paw through the garbage dump on the outskirts. They're searching for appetizing discards. Families come to watch. They park at a respectful distance and don't get out of their cars or trucks. Grizzlies don't like interference, from humans—or even from other bears.

In the dump, the king bear gets first dibs. The others let him pick out the prizes and keep away from the spots he chooses. Occasionally, a cocky young one invades the king's territory. He is given a thunderous growl and a boot with a paw that sends him rolling head over heels. He doesn't try that again. Sometimes the king will allow a favored female to share his feeding spot. But never another male. All the bears are clever with their paws. They pick up cans and drain them to the last smidgin if they like the contents. If they don't, they toss them. Their feeding time at the dump is a free circus.

It's not so funny when they steal food from somebody's freezer. Old hands at Kemano would never leave a freezer within their reach. But new arrivals, a young couple, once connected theirs in a doorless garage. Next morning, they found the top lifted off and all the steaks gone. The intruder left the rest. The bears are as choosy as they are strong.

Nancy's family freezer is stocked with cohoe, a form of salmon, from the Nechako River, which winds around Kemano. Nancy has won several prizes for catching the biggest cohoe of the season. She smokes and cans some of her catch every year. The river is only a few minutes walk from her house. She and her friends walk everywhere. Roads and family cars are few.

Her father flies to work in a "chopper," a helicopter. Walking, choppers, pick-up trucks and the boats that ply the long fjord snaking into Kemano from the Pacific Ocean, are Nancy's idea of transportation. She has never heard the honk of traffic or seen it jam a maze of big city streets. She's never scrambled for a bus, or been pushed in a rush-hour crowd. She can't really picture the numbers of students that catapult through big school corridors. The tempo and texture of city life is beyond her imagination. But teen-agers home from cities in the summer have told her enough to alarm her.

Nancy's Kemano is tiny. Normally about two or three hundred people live there. When construction is underway, however, the population swells, temporarily, into the thousands. The construction is powerhouse building. The powerhouse in Kemano was built inside a mountain in the 1950s by a work force of sixty-five hundred. The power it supplies is needed for the manufacture of aluminum in a big ALCAN (Aluminum Company of Canada) smelter in Kitimat. Aluminum, in tremendous world demand, is the reason for Kemano's existence.

The demand is so great that plans to build a second powerhouse are now afoot. The production of aluminum requires almost unbelievable amounts of power. The power used for a full five years by a home complete with every conceivable modern appliance would only be enough to make a single ton of this popular metal.

The present powerhouse is the product of turning nature upside down. In the beginning, engineers made the Nechako

River flow backwards. They reversed the flow with the biggest rock-filled dam in the world. They chopped down a mountain to get that much rock. When they finished, the Nechako River drained into lakes that once drained into it, forming a 358-square mile reservoir. Through a ten-mile tunnel, water then surged to the top of the mountain. From there, a cascade sixteen times the height of Niagara Falls boomed down inside. The force turned the turbines that spun the generators that produced the power.

Next question: how to transmit that power safely across mountains? Three of the first towers set up to support transmission lines were toppled by an avalanche in sixty seconds.

Engineers decided to perch the towers on peak tops and loop the lines in midair four thousand feet across from one to the other. How? Use a skyhook, was the joke in the construction camps strewn up and down the mountains.

The joke turned into a solution. Choppers with huge hooks lifted transmission towers in sections to twin summits. A bridge of narrow planks strung together was cranked up from the valley by a hoist, then noosed to six-foot-high bolts. These had been delivered to the peaks by choppers. Edging step by step across the dizzily swaying bridge, workmen strung lines between the towers.

Any Kemano boy or girl can tell you this story. They learn it in school, during one of the powerhouse study trips. Nancy has a badge from the Girl Guides, the Canadian Girl Scouts, for her report on the plant's history and operation. People in Kemano are proud of what has been accomplished.

The second powerhouse will require five or six years to build. To accomodate construction families, plans include a bigger school, a movie theater, an airport, a bowling alley. Temporary housing will be splattered across the neat community. There will be an RCMP, Royal Canadian Mounted Police unit. The people of Kemano are afraid that these increases will change their town.

"Our life will be spoiled, don't you see?" says Nancy. There will be a difference. Access to Kemano today is by an ALCAN helicopter going your way, by long boat passage which must be reserved well ahead of time, or by a small amphibian plane, which lands on the river. Fog and weather make schedules irregular. Kemano's spell is not broken by many outsiders. Nor is the community troubled by crime. Nobody locks doors. Only the grizzlies steal. People are quite comfortable with their own small security force.

Their fears of the future might just be needless, on account of those cohoe Nancy catches. Salmon swimming up river to spawn must have cool water. Water spilled out into rivers from power generators is hot. There are various ways of cooling the water and protecting the fish. ALCAN specialists have long pioneered in such projects. But they must satisfy the government of British Columbia that it can have both power and fish before any new construction can begin.

Meanwhile, the way Kemano is is good enough for Nancy. She meets her frog and geese friends at the outdoor swimming hole. In winter she uses an indoor heated pool, housed in a sizeable recreation center. There are tennis courts and a nine-hole golf course. The library she borrows from has five thousand well-thumbed books. Her home, surrounded by a landscaped yard, is hedged off from a gently winding street. Built of aluminum siding and painted in gentle pastels, the houses on her street are well spaced. Neighbors' noses don't poke into each other's barbecue grills.

Like many Kemano families, Nancy's has a small boat. In summer, she and her parents sail on the fjord for day picnics or weekend camping. If Nancy meets sea lions along the shore, she may toss them a fresh-caught fish. When she goes berry-picking, she passes one of the little streams beavers have dammed. The beaver family she knows has gnawed through small tree trunks to collect building material. If she wants to see the beavers, she makes a separate trip at night. Beavers sleep all day.

Another of her favorite spots is a camp at the end of a logging road that leads out of Kemano still farther into the wilderness. The road was bulldozed by EUROCAN, a company that gathers wood in the Kemano area. It is floated down-river to EUROCAN's Woodlands Headquarters, to be made into paper.

Loggers don't use the road after seven at night or over weekends. That's when Kemano people take over cabins that line the reservoir at the end of the road. The cabins are absolutely bare. Families bring fishing rods, sleeping bags, cooking gear and a few sundries. In spring they may not even need rods to catch a fine supper. Oolicans, which are sea smelt, spawn on the shores.

The cabins are scattered in a clearing surrounded by "dog-haired timber." That's the local name for hemlocks growing so thick there's no room for branches except at the top. The tops are umbrellas of shaggy fuzz. The trees climb partway up the mountains that, even in summer, are patched with stretches of snow, like polar bear rugs. Here and there, waterfalls mist down from melting snow.

Lips of snow curve on ridges between the mountains, as though smiling. In winter, those frozen smiles aren't to be trusted. Piled higher and higher by prevailing winds, they are the stuff from which avalanches are made. To protect trans-mission lines, choppers bomb the lips before they grow too big.

*An aerial view of an iron mine
at Ruth Lake, Quebec.*

The bombs have time fuses attached, so pilots can make a getaway before they explode.

Nancy has heard her father describe such missions. She knows that danger where she lives is danger that can be controlled. She feels safe. The young people who come home in summer talk of city dangers that are out of control. They tell tales of drugs and muggings. "You can't go out alone at night," they say. "I guess I lead a sheltered life," Nancy concludes.

The homecoming boys and girls agree. They hate to see their holidays end, though most of them work through the summer. Kemano has a vacation work program open to them and to university students from all British Columbia.

The pay for teen-agers isn't much—four dollars an hour—but when the return to Kemano is topped off with pay, these young people feel they have a real bonus. They clean up grounds, care for plants, cart off debris. They are out in open space once again. Twice a day they have coffee breaks, generally taken up with ongoing cribbage games. In the evenings, when work is done, they line the river, casting for cohoe.

University students who are studying engineering get jobs on transmission lines and in the powerhouse. Others run recreation programs for boys and girls. Their board and lodging is free. The work week is long—sixty hours—but the pay is good for temporary, unskilled labor, twenty-seven hundred dollars monthly. Some of them hope they can return, full time, when they graduate. Some who are growing up there have the same idea. "Women can be engineers," Nancy says. "Where better than here?"

CHAPTER **5**

Living in Town

THE TOWN OF KITIMAT THRIVES ON THE ALCAN SMELTER AND ERUOCAN's Woodlands paper plant. Boys and girls growing up there prefer the town type of action.

Late Saturday afternoon in June at the Mosdell home in a residential section of Kitimat, Father and a visiting uncle return from a day's fishing with a load of cohoe and crabs to clean. "Not in the kitchen," says mother, who is busy preparing for evening guests. They find a spot in the back yard overlooking a meadow and stream which divide their block from a shopping center. The front yard is currently occupied by the trailer tent that was hooked to Uncle's car when he drove his family there. On either side neighbors can almost look through the Mosdell's windows. That's how tight-packed the houses are.

Inside, the Mosdell home is roomy. It has to be. The eldest daughter is married, but two girls and a boy still live

59

*Kitimat families work together
to take down an old barn.*

with their parents: fifteen-year-old Jackie, her sister Debbie, who is fourteen, and brother Lee, seventeen. Every summer Uncle and Aunt come to visit with cousin Marcy, the youngest of the group. She's twelve.

At the moment, all are present and accounted for. Marcy is in the basement rumpus room playing chess with Lee. They are both chess hounds. Lee is at the same time listening to tapes through earphones. Perhaps because his attention is divided, Marcy is trouncing him. He makes a face, grunting. Jackie is playing the piano in the upstairs living room. Debbie is sprawled on the living room floor reading the advice to the lovelorn column in the local newspaper. Their aunt is helping their mother.

Shortly, the three girls are pressed into service, setting up for the supper guests. They lay out an assortment of chafing dishes and long forks. This will be a cook-your-own party, with an assortment of goodies, from spicy meatballs to the famous Pacific Ocean shrimp. Everybody dips his choice in one of a variety of piquant sauces. Boys and girls, as well as grown-ups are invited. It's a family affair.

Kitimat is partial to family parties. The day after theirs, the Mosdells go to a barn razing. The men tear down the barn boards. The boys and girls pull out the nails so the planks can be reused. The women prepare the barbecue, salad and a half-dozen pies. Everyone has brought some of the makings. When the barn is down and the last morsel of food relished, the stereo is switched on. Time to dance! The dancing lasts late into the night.

The lateness doesn't tire out Jackie, Debbie and Marcy. The morning after, they go rope swinging. The action begins with a scramble up a cliff in one of Kitimat's parks. At the peak a long, knotted rope is firmly secured. Grasping the

61

rope, they take turns swinging far out beyond the cliff. They let go in midair and drop into a cluster of balsam where the ground is softly blanketed with needles shed by the trees. "It's a motheree of a ride!" says Jackie. Motheree means humdinger or big blast. Western boys and girls use the expression frequently.

In the afternoon the three swim in a long arm of the Pacific that reaches into Kitimat. Though the beach is well kept, with benches and tables for picnicking, it doesn't get a great deal of use because of British Columbia weather. Summers are apt to be cloudy and rainy. The water is so cold that the sun is a necessity. June is generally sunny. Toward the end of the month, when the sun has had time to warm the water a little, everyone who can flocks to the beach. Lee Mosdell has a full-time summer job, so he is left out of the girls' fun.

When they can't swim in salt water, they use the heated indoor pool in the shopping mall across the meadow from their house. They took swimming lessons there when they were little. The lessons are part of a varied recreation program for young people, which is paid for by the town, but directed and operated entirely by volunteer parents. Kitimat's fourteen thousand people take a deep interest in youth affairs.

Many of these families have been attracted from other lands by job opportunities, principally with ALCAN and EUROCAN's Woodlands Headquarters. Among Debbie's, Jackie's and Lee's classmates are Portuguese, Italians, Finns, Germans, Greeks and East Indians. Debbie baby-sits for an East Indian family. With the money she earns, she buys her own school clothes.

She also has Canadian Indian friends, particularly Renata. She and Renata have studied and played together

since first grade. Their friendship has given her a clearer understanding of Indian problems than most of her white friends have. "It's true," Debbie says, "that Indians stare at you and ignore you if you try to talk to them. They act as though they are better than you." This is often said by white Canadian children. "But," Debbie adds, " there's a reason. Look, Indians were here first. They act stuck-up to show us they are the rightful owners."

She and Renata like to sketch together. Debbie works with charcoal. Her favorite subject is trees blowing in the wind. She has a knack for catching their sway. She also has an eye for fashion and spends a lot of her free time moseying in Kitimat's clothing specialty shops. When she graduates from high school, she means to go to work as a salesgirl in one of them. No college, she has decided. Eventually, she wants to marry and raise two or three children. But she's in no hurry. In the paperback romances she reads, young couples are always battling. Besides, she wants to travel some. But not too much. Even though she likes travel, she likes coming home even more. "I'll never leave Kitimat for good," she swears.

Her sister, Jackie, is just the opposite. She hopes to go to the University of Saskatchewan when she graduates, because the drama classes and theater complex there are famous throughout Canada. Theater is what Jackie's into. She has already attended a high school drama conference at the University of Victoria. Her school sponsored the trip, having chosen her as the "student most committed to theater" in her grade. She has friends who are also aiming for the University of Saskatchewan and the group has in mind to rent an apartment together. Summers, she wants to drive a truck, picking up and delivering goods. "That will let me travel and make money at the same time," she says.

63

An A student, Jackie keeps a sharp eye on material in all her classes that she can use in the drama courses she will take all through high school. In ancient history, she researches the art of make-up, which originated in Egypt. She practices as a speech exercise the tip-of-the-tongue pronunciation her French teacher demands. She likes the tripping sound. "I love French," she says. Many English-speaking Canadian children find it a bore. Jackie has related hers to what she wants to be.

Still, she's very much a girl of Kitimat. In the fall she goes with the family to gather logs for the huge fireplace in their living room. Dad and Lee chop. Mother and the two girls stack. They borrow a trailer to haul home their winter supply. The British Columbia Forest Service has designated the forest area where families may cut. Well before Christmas, they drive out again, searching for the shapeliest tree to decorate. The search date is becoming earlier and earlier, because the whole town combs the permitted sections and it's first come, best served.

Christmas vacation is toboggan time. By then, there's always plenty of snow, sometimes as much as sixteen feet. When it reaches the Mosdell roof, Dad digs a tunnel, so the children can get out to school and the grown-ups to work.

As in most Kitimat families, both parents work. Mr. Mosdell works for ALCAN and Mrs. Mosdell works for EUROCAN's Woodlands Headquarters. In the summer a good many teen-agers work for these companies. ALCAN is where Lee Mosdell works.

EUROCAN employs a well-spoken group of girls to guide guests through the plant where wood pulp is turned into paper. Seventeen year-old Kathy Williams is one of them. To learn her job, she took tours with the staff, then led practice tours with employees pretending to be visitors. Only, unlike visitors, they could and did correct Kathy's mistakes. After corrections, she had to be letter-perfect. Otherwise—no job. The money means a lot to her, because she's saving up for college.

The Mosdell girls took their cousin Marcy on one of Kathy's tours. What most fascinated Marcy was the use of baby salmon to test water that had been used to clean wood pulp. The wood pulp process takes a tremendous amount of water. The EUROCAN people like to return this water to its source, but they can only do so if they have removed pollution accumulated from the pulp. They do this with chemicals, then store the water for ninety-four hours in a baby salmon tank. If half the salmon live, the water's pure. In natural surroundings, fewer than half would survive. EUROCAN must give thought not only to the effect of a forestry harvest on the forest itself, but also on soil conservation, fish streams, watersheds and the wildlife of the woods.

The British Columbia Forest Service won't renew the license of any logging company that doesn't scrupulously mind these and other rules. But the service works hand in glove with loggers, because it knows that the healthiest forest are not those left to nature's whims; they are those cultivated by man. The province has the biggest and best forests in all Canada. Moreover, the lumber, paper and wood products, such as prefabricated homes, shipped annually from British Columbia to countries around the world earn enough to pay for half the services the provincial government provides. Forests help finance the Kitimat recreation program the Mosdell children enjoy.

Their cousin, Marcy, prefers a more citified type of activity, with rinks, arenas, crowds. She lives just outside

Edmonton, capital of the province of Alberta. Most recreation there is arranged by the Youth Association, which sends interviewers to Marcy's school every year to discuss what activities interest boys and girls most. The association sponsors a wide range, from arts and crafts to horseback riding. There's almost always some contest taking place in the huge sports arena, and the indoor roller skating rink is as crowded as are the outdoor winter ice skating rinks.

"It's slow here," says Marcy of Kitimat. Nevertheless, she likes to exchange city for country now and then. She has been writing poetry since she was six, and most often her poems are inspired by nature. Here is one about a forest waterfall:

> Cascades of tumbling, frothing indigo
>   over rocks, grinding, smoothing
>   like a diligent mason forever working.
> Sparkling and shining in the sunlight,
>   bubbling and babbling joyously
>   in the quiet peaceful forest.
> Crystal clear, cold and colorful
>   spraying droplets, shining prisms,
>   rainbows gracing waters,
>   waters gracing rainbows.
> Water falling
>   tumbling
>   diving
>   over the edge, acrobatic,
>   into the deep, still, quiet pool,
>   dark, peaceful, calm.

Boys and girls in all Canada, whether they live in towns like the Mosdells, or cities like Marcia, like to escape to the country. This is especially true in the west and is even so if a town is practically in the country already. Mayo, in the Yukon, is such a town.

A Mayo family leaves its log cabin, or trailer, or aluminum siding, or modern split-level home and less than ten minutes later is out of sight of any human existence. Left behind is the hodgepodge of construction that shelters 900 or so people in whatever kind of housing they can afford. The family van or truck bumps through a landscape of lakes, giant spruce and sharp-peaked mountains. The car is loaded with children. They are almost a third of Mayo's small population.

Elsewhere than Canada, Mayo might be called a village, but in Canada the population is so scattered that each cluster assumes more than life-size importance. Village-sized communities become towns; towns are promoted to cities. The town of Mayo has a special distinction. It's a Local Improvement District, known as LID. As such, Mayo receives government funds to help keep roads, public buildings, and general appearance in order. There are only three workers on the LID staff, but they have every man, woman and child in town behind them. In the spring, when the snow disappears, school closes for a day to let students join the annual LID cleanup of under-snow debris. Each boy and girl receives a big plastic garbage bag, plus a bag of potato chips and a can of fruit juice for refreshment on the way.

The result of this public-private cooperation is that little Mayo is a model town when compared with the seedy, tumble-down look of many other Yukon communities its size, or even larger. Some of the public buildings are just Quonset huts, but they shine. Small yards are primped with flowers in the short summer. Paint doesn't peel from houses. The people of Mayo spell tidiness with a capital T.

Their enterprise attracts other settlers in the trucking and distribution businesses. Mayo is a center for receiving and dispatching goods in its part of the Yukon. As more people move in, Mayo merchants seize on the chance to make money by serving them. Some Yukon towns twice Mayo's size are lucky to have a single grocery store. Mayo has three, one of which specializes in top grade meats, hard to come by in the Yukon.

Michael Mason-Wood, thirteen, and his ten year-old sister Charyl, nicknamed "Charlie," are the children of the North Star Motel keeper. Their father runs a busy, well-kept set of lodgings, which he has built on top of the family home. The Mason-Woods are among those who benefit from Mayo's caretaking.

Back of their home is a vegetable and flower garden, raspberry patch, picnic table and the small greenhouse so often put up by families in the northwest. The antlers of a moose Michael shot are perched on the roof gable over the back door. He also hunts grouse and duck, when he isn't busy fishing. Smoked fish and moose are two of Charlie's and Michael's favorite foods.

Both children help plant and weed the garden. They start seedlings in boxes indoors in March, so as to give them a headstart. Michael also helps his dad in the motel. Summertimes, he works loading and unloading luggage at Mayo's little airport. His pay goes into his college savings account. Charlie salvages deposit bottles and turns them in for pin money. Guests leave a lot of them in the motel.

Both have their collections. Charlie has twenty-five teddy bears and Michael has thirty-five billed work hats, imprinted with the names of companies or places. The work cap is popular summer headgear with western Canadian boys. The most prized are those with the names of companies that have gone out of business, because then the cap can't be duplicated anymore. It's status.

Another of the Mason-Woods' hobbies is making things with their hands. They have built a flock of model cars and little birchbark canoes. Charlie presses flowers and butterflies, then frames them. Such craftwork occupies long winter nights, along with their favorite indoor sport: toy car racing. They have a track and each owns two cars which they race intently, but without quarreling. Brother and sister are good friends.

The whole family collects rocks. They do their searching mostly on summer camping trips. They have camped their way to Vancouver and Los Angeles. Once they camped all across Canada. Michael isn't keen on camping too far south in the summer. "The daylight doesn't last," he complains. He is used to the sunny summer nights of the north.

Most of their trips are short ones, because the family is so busy. The short trips are weekends or overnights in the woodsy lake and mountain area around Mayo. Their aunt and uncle have a cabin on Ethel Lake and a power boat. They take Michael and Charlie water skiing. Sometimes the two visit the Taylors, friends from Seattle, Washington, who have a summer home above Mayo Lake. Troy Taylor is close to Michael's age and Tammy Taylor and Charlie are only a few years apart. Mrs. Taylor is American and Mr. Taylor Canadian. The young Taylors therefore have dual citizenship. When they reach eighteen they will have to decide whether they prefer to be American or Canadian.

On a solitary plateau above the lake, the Taylors have perched an A-Frame, a mini-trailer and a collapsible hexagon of screening with a plastic roof that serves as an outdoor

69

dining area. The plateau is just barely big enough for these shelters and a visitor's truck. Mr. and Mrs. Taylor make jewelry, with the children's help. They have lodged a small sluice, a trough blocked by a gate, in a stream that tumbles down one side of the plateau. With this contraption they can usually collect enough gold for their work. They sell the jewelry in Seattle in the winter.

Every two weeks or so in summer, Michael and Charlie spend a night with them. Betweentimes, the Taylor children visit the Mason-Woods. When Charlie's and Michael's parents can't drive them to the camp, they ride their bikes from town, turning off on a rutted, twisting dirt road that bumps up hill and down. But wide-branched spruce, guarding the edges, keep it dusky-cool. The Taylor place is a kind of secret hideaway. You have to know it's there to find it.

Summer weekdays Michael and Charlie swim in their town pool and play baseball. The teams are mixed: both boys and girls play on the same team. Fortunately, Michael has time for sports, because he has to be at the airport only when planes arrive and depart. The other hours are all his own.

There's as much to do outdoors in winter as in summer. Hockey teams—mixed, as in baseball—keep up a running combat. Snowmobiles whiz over the countryside. Sometimes Mr. Mason-Wood attaches a rope to the rear of his Ski-Doo. Charlie or Michael, on skis, holds onto the rope and is towed behind. When Michael drives the Ski-Doo, Charlie isn't crazy about skiing behind him. Once he went so fast she crashed and broke her skis.

Charlie has an unfailing aim with a snowball and is in great demand in snowball fights. Teams build snow walls and duck behind them, standing up to throw. A player who is hit is out. The fight lasts until one of the two teams has been knocked out entirely.

Charlie also likes snow hide-and-go-seek. The players bury themselves in the snow. The one who's "it" has to guess their whereabouts from the way the snow looks. Is that mound just another snowdrift, or is there somebody underneath? Charlie thrusts her snowshoe in to find out. If she hits somebody, he's "it."

Charlie's friend, eleven year-old Pauline Drapeau, who lives in a split-level home across town from the North Star Motel, likes this game, too, but she prefers summer to winter on account of the camping. She's expert at pitching the family tent and she enjoys catching and helping prepare camp food. She does all the fishing and filets and cleans her catch. She can also skin the rabbits she snares. They compete with smoked fish for the top spot on her favorite list of foods.

Her brother, twelve year-old Louis, helps her gather the wood for cooking, but he loathes camping, especially when there's rain. When asked how long the family camps, his answer is glum: "As long as we can stand it." Pauline corrects: "As long as *you* can stand it."

Louis likes the fresh fish his sister catches, but he hates the smoked variety. He prefers winter to summer, even though his winter household chore is to "pack" groceries. Packing means hitching a rope around a train of boxes and pulling them, on foot, over ice and snow.

Winter gives Louis time for his woodwork. He makes planters and builds shelves and cabinets. They are all beautifully finished. He has learned some of the skills that underlie his artistry in industrial arts, his favorite subject in school.

For his favorite game, he has to wait for summer, however.

71

It's called murder ball. Two balls are placed between two teams. Each team rushes to grab them. The object is to hit an opponent with a ball, whereupon, he's sent to "prison." He can be released if another member of his team retrieves a ball, gives it to him, and he hits a member of the enemy team. The player who is hit must then take the prisoner's place in jail. The winning team succeeds in jailing all the others. The game can go on for hours, sometimes with a lunch or supper, or even overnight, break. No team ever quits until the very end.

All year round, Louis and Pauline make their specialties for the family menu. They are both good cooks. Pauline bakes bread, pies, cakes and pastry. She prepares the vegetables from the corner of the garden that she plants and tends. Louis broils chicken, fries French toast for breakfast and stuffs and roasts the Christmas turkey. "Louis eats all the time," Pauline says. "No," retorts Louis, "I only eat a lot."

Pauline would like to live in a bigger town one day. There are plenty of different sorts for her to choose from. Because, except around a very few big cities, there are no long strings of highway-connected, look-alike communities. And because Canada has more space than towns, the distances between them preserve their separate personalities.

Part of the personality of the Québec town of Gaspé on the Atlantic coast is its annual homecoming parade. For a week in mid-July, festivities break out all over to welcome Gaspésians returning for visits from other parts of Canada. That's the excuse for the gaiety, but the eighteen thousand who have never moved away look forward to the week just as much as their guests. Fifteen-year-old David Eden won a prize in one of the parades for masquerading as an old-time pioneer. He cut pines to make a mock forest which he set up in the back of his father's truck. He persuaded the local museum to lend him an ancient muzzle-loader gun. He copied his costume from a picture in a library book. He set up a log table and tent stove in the shade of his forest, and was driven along brewing tea and baking bread.

David had to fit the work of readying his float into off-hours from his summer job as a playground helper and his volunteer leadership of Cub Scouts. He canoes, hikes and camps with the Cubs in the summer. Most of his charges are French Canadian. David is an English Canadian. He can understand French, but not yet speak a great deal of it. His Québecois friends are helping him to learn. "The trouble with most English," he says, "is they don't *try* to learn." He continues: "Québec *is* French. No use to fight that. If you've got a point to make—speak it, but not with your fists." He has seen English-French fist fights, of which he heartily disapproves.

When he disapproves, others are apt to listen. He is a strapping athlete, big for his age. Until he suffered a knee injury, he was sought after as a goalie in hockey. His height helps him excel at basketball. He sails a skiff with a friend and fishes and hunts, going after partridge, rabbit, and especially deer. The whole family is keen on venison, which David, Mother, Dad, also two younger brothers know how to cook to perfection. Sometimes David supplies venison as one of the meats that load the tables at the family's twin Christmas dinners.

"At noon we eat with Mother's parents and at night with Dad's, or the other way 'round," he explains. What do they eat? Roast pork, ham, turkey, maybe the venison, potatoes, turnips, carrots, cole slaw, cranberry sauce, plum pudding. There's a lot of eating the week before, too, at spur-of-the-moment parties. "Someone brings a guitar, someone brings a

Families in town and villages
also play together.

violin, everyone brings some food and we sing and dance and eat until we have to sleep," is how David describes these happenings.

At the beginning of the week, David chooses a Christmas tree to cut from the slope of the mountain above his home. He tows the tree down with a rope attached to the family Ski-Doo. In summer, he plants and tends the family garden. His help is essential, since both his parents work; his mother as a receptionist in the town motel and his father as a sales parts manager for the Canadian branch of an American automobile manufacturer. They depend on David.

When his parents get their vacations, they take David and his brothers to other Canadian provinces. David has now visited every Canadian province except Newfoundland. His favorite is British Columbia. "Because of the mountains and the forests," he says. His own province has these, too, but the Laurentians of Québec have been more rounded by grinding glaciers during the ice age, and the forests are not as thick and abundant. He would like to return to British Columbia, and he hopes to complete his tour of the provinces with a trip to Newfoundland. For David, "travel is part of education."

CHAPTER 6

Going to School
in Town and Country

DAVID GOES TO SCHOOL IN GASPÉ'S C. E. POULIOT POLYVALENTE. The *polyvalente* is a special kind of secondary school, which, in Canada, is found only in the province of Québec. The name means many values, and that's exactly what a polyvalente offers. The choice of what values students want to acquire— in other words, what courses they want to take—are largely their own. They must study French, English and math. After that they choose studies by the group, whether science, art, literature and social studies, or perhaps business or vocational courses. Not only among such groups, but within each one, boys and girls have such a wide selection of subjects that the polyvalente has been called a shopping center for education.

It's a shopping center that appeals to students and attracts young teachers with talent and imagination. Maurice Joncos, David Eden's teacher in a course called communication (meaning composition) is one of this modern breed. He

76

*Katia Garon at her desk at
school in Quebec City.*

turns the work of writing a composition into an adventure by sending his students out, like reporters, to cover their subjects.

"From today on," he tells them in his opening class, "nothing is going to escape us, whether politics, sports, history, here in Gaspé, or worldwide." He cites, as possible stories, sports matches scheduled to take place, tensions in Québec's relationship with the federal government, tensions in the Middle East. He suggests sources for keeping up with events: television programs, newspapers—among the latter the distinguished American *New York Times*, which can be found in the school's well-stocked library.

Since most of his students are French Canadians, an assignment to read in English might be expected to call forth groans. Not at all. Maurice Joncos turns such assignments into challenges. The boys and girls in his class are excited by the opportunity. They feel they are being introduced to "The age of information," a phrase they have learned from him. They want to succeed in this new age.

The school serves some eighteen hundred students who bus from a forty-mile radius around Gaspé. On the last lap, the buses climb the bluff where the school overlooks the sea. From the windows of almost every classroom, a broad expanse of Atlantic Ocean is visible. New arrivals will spend five years in these pleasant surroundings.

They arrive at a polyvalente with six grades of elementary education behind them. But in the polyvalente, grade levels lose much of their importance. Students pass subjects, not grades. At Pouliot a student will tell you what "family" he belongs to, instead of what grade he's in. Every student is assigned to a school family group.

The system is meant to make the atmosphere of a large school as personal as can be. Each family has its own director

78

and its own round of duties and activities. Members can put forward ideas without feeling lost in a crowd. Students believe the system gives them a hand in helping to run their school.

In spite of the number of students, there's very little commotion in the corridors. Students move freely about, but without much hurtling, pushing or shoving. In the carrefours, some of them smoke between classes. Smoking is permitted in certain areas of most Québecois secondary schools, though never in classrooms. The principal of the Pouliot school would like to outlaw smoking, but it's doubtful that he can succeed. Many teenagers smoke with their parents at home. Neither they nor their parents see any reason why not in school. And when personal habits are at stake, the Québecois is highly particular about his rights.

The principal would also like to persuade his teachers of English to speak only English in their classes. By law, however, they are not forced to do so before grade nine. Consequently, with some outstanding exceptions, below that grade English is taught in French.

The same thing happens to French in the Protestant schools, which are attended almost entirely by English-speaking Canadians. French is taught in English. The Protestant school is a product of a system under which, in Québec and some of the other provinces, education is administered by religious groups. In Newfoundland, for example, three different ones are in charge. Anglicans, the United Church and Roman Catholics.

Usually the groups share the same building, but sometimes the buildings are separate. No matter, the subjects studied are the same all over a province. So are the textbooks. The provincial government supplies these and all classroom materials. It pays the teachers and other school staff. Religious denominations contribute to building maintenance, or, if they want separate buildings, they bear the cost of construction. In the Pouliot Polyvalente, Protestant and Catholic schools share the same building, which is a relatively new one.

This modern school is a symbol of the progress Québec is making since the Official Languages Act helped improve job opportunities for Québecois. The Gaspé peninsula used to be considered *defavorisé*—underprivileged. All the way out into the ocean, the coastline was pocked with tumbledown villages, lucky to have a one-room schoolhouse. In some, children begged in the streets, or hawked needlework and crudely carved miniature boats. They were raggedly dressed. Their education was so poor that they could barely read and write.

Today, in one such town, Grand Rivière, new houses have almost entirely replaced weatherbeaten cottages. At evening, the cove they border, sheltered by jutting cliffs, is crowded with homecoming fishing boats, motored, well-painted, laden with the day's catch. Most of the townsmen fish, or work in other sections of the fishing industry, or are employed in interior forests. Some manage two jobs. Grand Rivière—like other Gaspé towns—is growing steadily, and its schools—two fine ones—reflect that growth.

Sister Mary Bouchard presides over the elementary school. She is also the English teacher—and not one of those who tries to teach it in French. Not a word of French escapes her lips in English class, nor will she permit any relapse from any pupil. They don't mind, because there are so many English games to play, comic books to read, tapes to listen to, songs to sing, crossword puzzles to solve.

The class begins with boys and girls breaking into song

about "this is the way we wash our hands, clean our teeth, comb our hair, at eight o'clock in the morning." They sing their way through a day's activities at different hours until the song ends with "this is the way we go to bed," and all heads collapse on the desks. The singing is accompanied by pantomine that belongs with the activity.

Boys and girls may also suggest verses. One boy brought his pet rabbit to class in a box, let him loose and sang out: "This is the way we catch a rabbit," whereupon the whole class gave chase.

Even without rabbits, Sister Bouchard's classes are rarely still. They dance to some of their songs, march to others. The quieter games, too, can challenge inventiveness. In one, the class plans a trip across Canada. In another, they complete crossword puzzles from pictures. That is, instead of words in the horizontal and vertical listings there are pictures. Then, in the puzzle squares, pupils supply the English words that describe the pictures. When Sister Bouchard's students enter her room, they never know what surprise the day will bring. No wonder English is their favorite subject!

They will be more than usually prepared in it when they go to the Grand Rivière Polyvalente up the hill. The Polyvalente is new. On opening day, students and teachers walked out together, after taking one look at the cement block walls, painted over, inside and out, in gray. Gray is not the Québec idea of how a school should look. A jail, maybe, but not a school. Canadians love color and no Canadian loves it more than a Québecois. The elementary school building in Grand Rivière is an old one, but it's alive with color, shocking pink, purple, daffodil yellow. Teachers weren't about to teach, or pupils about to study in the depressing atmosphere of the new polyvalente.

The walkout did it. Painters were hastily dispatched with buckets of contrasting shades. Overnight, doors stood out in brilliant hues. Next, walls were coated. Students contributed the carrefour murals, seascapes with boats and gulls. Parents also took brushes in hand.

Parent-student-teacher cooperation is strong in many schools across Canada. In the École Saint Dominique in Québec City, the relationship is especially close. Saint Dominique boys and girls come from a variety of backgrounds. Mexicans, East Indians, Africans, children from Central Europe sit side by side with French Canadians. Their parents work side by side at volunteer jobs.

From this international base, the school opens windows on the world. It mounts displays showing the work of the United Nations. Exhibits and concerts by artists and musicians from abroad are a regular part of Saint Dominique's year. So are opportunities for contact with young Canadians in other provinces. Students can join an interprovince pen pal club. They can also have exchange visits.

Saint Dominique is one of a great and growing number of Canadian schools that takes advantage of wide-ranging opportunities for exchanges. Students as young as eleven and on up through high school can spend anywhere from a few days to several months, or even a year, depending on how old they are, living with families and going to school in other parts of the country. This is the way the boys and girls of isolated Fermont, in Labrador, get to know the life of Québec City. The visits are arranged by both government and private agencies, or the two in cooperation. For older students, there are also exchanges with the United States, and some with Europe. The greater part of a student's expense is usually paid by the sponsoring organization.

At Saint Dominique, when extra money is needed for any cause, it is raised by parents and students. When school opens in the fall, students set out on a "neighborhood march." From each house they request whatever people can afford to give. The contributions are usually generous, because school affairs are always open to neighbors and are well attended. Student-raised funds are deposited in a local bank where they earn interest. The bank adds a contribution to their earnings.

Parents hold fund-raising affairs as well as making and collecting personal donations. These funds are used not only for educational activities but also for just plain fun. There are class parties and a school-wide feast when Père Noël (Father Christmas) visits school. He arrives in the city by parachute.

Parents and students also work at school chores. Parents guard the school entrance. Boys and girls serve as marshals, helping fellow students cross the busy street where the school is located, and regulating corridor traffic inside. The marshals wear bright red shoulder straps and a bright red belt, to which their official badge is attached. They are selected for *"la soucie de groupe,"* concern for all. The selection is made by the principal and teachers from recommendations submitted by students. The marshal's job, the principal makes clear, is to help, not supervise others. They act accordingly.

Katia Garon, part Mexican, part Indian, is a captain of the marshals. Her father has charge of records on the geology of the Laurentian Mountains, so occasionally Katia has a chance for a climb. She almost drew a mountain on her desk sign, but decided she would rather have something amusing. All the Saint Dominique pupils make desk signs with their names and original drawings. Some have flowers; some have

83

the moon and stars; some have the sun and clouds; some have boats on the Saint Lawrence River, which flows alongside their city. On hers, Katia drew a turtle wearing one of the little red hats Québec City people don for their winter carnival. Sometimes the hat may be yellow, or it may be a white stocking cap. Katia likes the red ones best.

At carnival time in February, there's a long parade, headed by a queen and six duchesses commanding their followers. In front of the queen a jolly seven-footer marches, dressed as a snowman with a bright red sash and a tasseled cap, which gives him a Santa-like appearance. If the Saint Lawrence River is frozen solid, iceboats race across its expanse. If the ice is slushy, canoes struggle through the floes. The river banks are lined with spectators, cheering their favorite craft.

The boys and girls of Saint Dominique join in the street decoration that turns the city into a snow sculpture museum for carnival. Yards, fence posts, walls, sprout with heads and full figures of people, animals and angels—whatever strikes a sculptor's imagination. These snow models are carefully iced over, and barring an early thaw, last for the two weeks of goings-on. Neighbor rivals neighbor and block rivals block to see who can produce the most fantastic effects. Katia's sculpture outside Saint Dominique was a turtle, like the one on her desk sign. Some of her classmates built a castle.

From time to time Katia and other pupils may be invited to the principal's office. They don't quake and shake. They look forward to the candy. The principal pushes toward them the jar that's always on her desk and they help themselves. Likely as not, they are asked for advice on some problem or project in the school. Pupils' opinions are often sought on school affairs.

In the Louis Riel Polyvalente in Montréal, the province's largest city, student's opinions are also sought. Their school, which serves some two thousand boys and girls, was built at a cost of more than eight million dollars. This sum was spent to provide an enticing array of opportunities for work and play—from a twelve thousand-volume library to twelve tennis courts. The sports facilities, including lighted soccer, baseball and football fields, shaking rinks and four gyms, are open to the neighborhood evenings.

As in the Pouliot school in Gaspé, the large student body is organized in smaller units. At Louis Riel three sections are divided into groups of only thirty each. The groups of thirty do everything together throughout their school career, including a week of skiing in the Laurentians on school time and a "green week," which is a spring trip to countryside or seashore.

One such group has as their English teacher Michel Mathieu, who runs his class like a show, with the audience taking part. Speaking only English, he uses pantomime to illustrate his meaning. Discussing test results, he remarks, "Some of you flipped," and tosses a coin to explain the expression. As he hands back the papers, he offers comments: "That's pretty cool," or "Your brother did better than you did." He questions a great deal, drawing pupils into dialogue. For instance: "Suppose you got mad at me and punched me in the nose, what would happen?"

"I'd get kicked out of school."

"Then what would you do?"

"Get a job."

"What kind of a job?"

"An easy one."

"Why easy?"

"Because I'm lazy."

"So you finally admit it. But you shouldn't. You don't want to destroy your reputation."

The class laughs heartily. While enjoying the performance, students learn English. They are not afraid to turn the tables on their teacher, either. Once, when he asked them to tell him who had a lovely voice because he wanted someone to read out loud, the answer came in unison—"YOU!"

So he read. But the last laugh was still his, for at the end of the tale, classmates had to take turns retelling the story.

While not every teacher is gifted with the art of dramatizing lessons, the trend for drama is growing in Canadian classrooms. In the Courtland Park School in a Montréal suburb, math may be used to play a game of politics. The school is Protestant and English speaking. One of the math lessons requires students to put together government budgets. Ginette Bergevin, the teacher, pretends to be the provincial premier. The students are ministers in charge of departments. They have to present the premier with budgets for department needs. Sometimes the game takes an unexpected turn. In one opening explanation, the teacher pointed out that if the department of education had no money, students would have no teachers, no books, no schools. The class cheered.

Students of French in the Courtland Park School have a chance to enroll in what is called an immersion program. "Immersion" means to be wholly ducked under water, head and all, but in the case of this program, the ducking is in French. For the first three grades all subjects are taught only in French, and after that sixty percent are in French. During ski weeks or green weeks, immersion students speak only French all day long. The program is new and popular in an increasing number of Canadian provinces, from coast to coast. There's apt to be a waiting list of candidates for schools that have it.

In the Jeanne Leber primary school in Montréal, which has a great many English and other non-French-speaking students, French is taught with a point system. The points are won in games. In the biography game, for example, boys and girls give short talks about their lives. The class votes on how many points each speaker should receive. In the vocabulary game, the teacher writes a letter of the alphabet on the board. Students see how many words they can come up with, beginning with that letter. There's a point for every word.

The point system also applies to other subjects. At Christmastime, the student with the most points wins five dollars, the one with the next most four dollars, and so on down to a dollar. The game recommences in the second term, with new awards at graduation time.

Even in such schools, however, the likelihood is that they will not learn the French language as it is spoken in France. The great majority of French teachers in all Canadian schools are Québec born. French in Québec and in France today are vastly different in sound, and sometimes in vocabulary. Only the basic grammar is the same.

The French of Québec is still spoken much as the explorers and colonists of the sixteenth century spoke it when they opened up and settled the land. But those pioneers would be very much surprised to hear the added influence of some tones and terms that come from English. One of these is "le fun." Thus, an enthusiastic Louis Riel student refers to ski week as *"ben* le fun." "Ben" is a Québecois contraction of the French word *"bien,"* meaning much, good, well.

Never mind. French in Canada is taught as it is spoken

in Canada, and in this, as in other subjects, many teachers merit stars. Canadian parents want the best possible education for their children and they are willing to work and pay for it. Consequently, most provinces have been able to attract high quality teachers by offering high salaries and security on the job. Usually, a job, though not necessarily the same one, is guaranteed from the day a teacher first sets foot in his or her classroom. There's no waiting period for that certainty. But there's a long period of training before a young person becomes eligible for such a job—up to ten years of study and preparation after graduating from secondary school. The time varies somewhat from province to province, but in general, boys' and girls' teachers are as thoroughly trained as they are rewarded. That's why so many boys and girls can expect to find adventure in their classrooms.

Perhaps the most adventure-filled school in all Canada is at Carcross, about 300 miles south of Mayo, in the Yukon Territory. Called "The Carcross Community," it was founded by an Anglican Bishop, the Right Reverend John Frame, who wanted "to give urban kids an introduction to frontier life," and a chance "to acquire real knowledge of their own weaknesses and skills." With church funds he bought and repaired a group of run-down buildings. Students themselves made further improvements. They come to Carcross from cities all over the country, but their numbers are kept small, with one teacher for every three of them.

The students sign contracts promising to perform tasks that range from kitchen chores and manning the boiler to building maintenance, sanitation, financial administration, farming and hunting. Teachers, called "parent members," serve more for love than pay. The latter is small.

The school is completely self-sufficient. Trained in the

use of a rifle, students hunt caribou and moose for food, raise chickens and pigs, bake bread, grow and preserve vegetables. What they can't use, they sell. Their plump, grainy bread is a best-seller in the area. They learn how to cut trees and split logs. Some logs are used to heat the community, the rest sold for railroad ties to a local railroad, with which they have a ten thousand dollar-a-year contract.

Work on these projects isn't allowed to interrupt a full high school schedule of classroom studies and homework. So the work day is long and weekends aren't time off. But this busy life seems to agree with the community's members. When seventeen-year-old Peter Breene from a big city school in Ontario graduated from the community, he summed up a general feeling: "My old school had twenty-five hundred kids, bells, no humanization. Here . . . there's preparation for life . . . I'll go on to college with solid experience in plumbing and lots more patience."

Private funds made Peter's experience possible. Not only private schools like Peter's, but in some cases provincial public schools also benefit from nongovernment support. One forward-looking source of such support is the Canada Studies Foundation. As one of its ventures the foundation helps finance courses that focus on today's problems in city living. A section of this project, called "Canada West" has become popular with both students and teachers in that part of the country. Committees of teachers, sometimes with student advice, map out topics for investigation. In Calgary, Alberta, several classes are looking into what happens to farmers who become city dwellers. In a Calgary suburb, the topic is the tactics of pressure groups. At the Britannia School in Vancouver, British Columbia, students study slums. In Winnipeg, Manitoba, ten- to twelve-year-olds are learning what it's like to be an Indian child their age in their city. In Saskatoon, Saskatchewan, Grownskill School pupils are digging into conflicts between hanging on to one's own lifestyle and winning acceptance in a do-as-the-rest-do society. A number of western schools are examining the effects of sudden city growth. Others are charting the ways, both good and bad, in which cities grow.

Such studies, using the methods of good newspaper reporters, help boys and girls explore new horizons. The sense of fresh discovery is one of the few constants found in most classrooms across the country, though how much it's developed varies. The fact is that courses, grades, indeed almost every aspect of school life vary so sharply in the ten provinces and two territories that the Canadian system of education can't be described as a whole. There are twelve systems, not one. And there is no federal office of education. Even when the federal government wants to help schools with money, the offer has to be made at the back door. That is, first the federal parliament passes a law encouraging "regional development," for example, under which heading it can then earmark grants for courses in related subjects. But provinces that accept grants can't be forced to spend them on what parliament suggests. They can spend the money any way they like.

The greatest similarity among schools is the number of years boys and girls attend; generally eleven, six in elementary grades, five in secondary grades. But don't depend on that. Some schools, like those in Ontario have thirteen grades. Some offer a seventh year in elementary school for students in need of extra study; some an extra high school year for college preparation. A few have junior high schools.

The subject matter differs widely. In some provinces, schools teach metric math, in others regular math. In some provinces language courses, especially French, are skimpy, but

90

in British Columbia the number of students in French classes increased four times between 1968 and 1980. Under the official Languages Act, that province accepted a grant for teaching French—and used it for that purpose.

Some provinces pay little attention to courses in history and geography; some pay a great deal. In few, however, do boys and girls learn much history of their own country. Groups of educators have called for more attention to Canadian history, but with little result. They have also made countless suggestions for making school programs across the country more alike—also without success.

Meanwhile, boys and girls who have to move from one province to another often find themselves in deep trouble in school. They are likely to be out of step with their new classmates, either behind or ahead, to know more or less than the others, to be lost in a new way of teaching an old subject. There are increasing numbers of such boys and girls, because their fathers, especially engineering fathers, are so frequently moved from job site to job site. In one year alone, 1977 to 1978, one hundred thousand students switched schools. Twenty thousand of these came to British Columbia. They accounted for five per cent of the province's school enrollment. Imagine the struggle of a student fresh from a province where little French is taught landing over his head in one of British Columbia's in-depth French classes! Imagine, on the other hand, the boredom of a student repeating in a new high school what he had already learned in a junior high or seventh grade in his old school. Or sympathize with the confusion of the young person who has had only regular math and sees metric math on the blackboard—or perhaps has to make an equally confusing change from metric to regular.

Another school problem springs largely from the severity

The giant ice figure of
Bonhomme Carnaval sits in a
downtown square in Quebec
City during winter carnival.

of Canadian winters and the high price of fuel. The more pupils per building, the fewer buildings are needed and the lower the heating costs. So, especially in rural areas in central and western Canada, a growing number of schools serving just a few hundred pupils, or sometimes less, are being closed. Their students are bussed to the nearest big school, where, willy-nilly, if room doesn't already exist, it's made for them. Their welcome depends on their numbers and the size of the bigger school. If facilities are overburdened, the welcome may be cool. Also the "nearest" school may be located at a considerable distance, requiring long travel, sometimes with transfers from one bus to another. Most of the schools affected by the closings are elementary schools. Committees of parents have actively opposed what they consider too great a hardship for young children, but they haven't been able to come up with solutions for the root of the problem: costs.

Nevertheless, from the point of view of most Canadian boys and girls, the advantages of their schools are greater than the drawbacks. They are more apt to enjoy than to gripe about their classes. In a country of long and lonely distances, school is a get-together place—the place where the action is.

CHAPTER **7**

Working and Playing
in the Maritimes

FOURTEEN-YEAR-OLD MARIA CONNORS, DREAMS ABOUT HER school in Rexton New Brunswick, while she paints the backyard fence in summer. Her nearest girlfriends live five miles away. They ride their bikes to visit each other, but actually, they meet more often on the school bus in winter than biking in summer. Maria's father has to leave their remote, hilltop home at six in the morning to reach his job at a trailer and prefab factory in the nearest small town. He doesn't return until seven at night. Even grocery shopping takes an eighty-mile round trip drive.

In the next few years, Maria will probably have more neighbors. New roads are being carved out around her and small houses being built. The prefab factory is doing a booming business. The Connorses themselves have a new house going up behind their present one. Although New Brunswick has developed more slowly than some of the other

*Peter van Schaick with the
driftwood he and his brother
mistook for a drowning deer.*

Maritimes, the name for the provinces that border the Atlantic Ocean, it's now making up for lost time.

Maria is both a winner and a worker. Besides winning her school beauty contest, she has been the queen of the local snow carnival. One Halloween she was awarded first prize for a gypsy costume, although she thought an earlier disguise as Dracula was more dramatic.

When the season arrives for the local agricultural fair, the fair committee comes to Maria for help in collecting contributions to pay for the tents and booths where animals and garden produce are displayed. Maria has the reputation of being able to collect the most money of anybody in the area.

At home, she helps care for the vegetable garden, freezes the crops for winter fare and shares all the cooking with her mother. She's been cooking since she was seven and is now an expert in the kitchen. One of her favorite dishes is *torta rustica*, a high, puffy pastry, stuffed with spinach, cottage cheese and egg, well spiced.

She built the fence she keeps painted, including digging the holes for the fence posts. She drives a tractor for her uncle, who runs a cattle farm across the road, helps him with the haying and with cutting wood in the forest. Sale of the wood pays for extra cattle feed. Her uncle's acreage isn't big enough, nor the rocky soil rich enough to produce all the cattle require. Few Maritime farmers can make ends meet by farming alone. Most of them do other work as well. In New Brunswick, cutting wood for pulp mills is often the life saver.

Maria earns money for doing her share of the family chores. She saves what she earns for car insurance and college. Her parents will let her use the family car when she's old enough to get a license, but she will have to pay the extra amount the insurance will then cost. She will also need to contribute to the expense of college, particularly if she goes to a university abroad, as she would like to do. She has developed a taste for travel from her family's trips to England and Italy.

Her mother was Italian born, and her father, though born in New Brunswick, spent many years in England. He came home to help his brother with the cattle farm. Maria's mother lived through a terrible time of bombing in Italy during the Second World War. The people of her town, Monte Casino, were ordered to leave their homes. They lived in a cave until the bombs ceased. When they returned, they found out why the bombing had stopped. Nothing was left.

When she was able, the young girl who was to be Maria's mother left Italy for England, where she had obtained a job with a family, taking care of a child. There, she met the man she married. Maria was born in England, but she has lived in New Brunswick since she was four.

Her first trip to Italy was solo, when she was eight. Her parents put her on the plane; her relatives met her when the plane landed. She lived with them for a month, helping pick their tomato crop. She looks forward to the return trips the whole family generally takes to Italy and England once a year.

Having been born in England, with a Canadian father, Maria, like the Taylor children, has dual citizenship. At eighteen she can attend a university in either Canada or England, depending on her choice of nationality. But Maria wants to go to a university in Switzerland! She also wants to travel around the world.

World travel is one of the dreams she spins while working or playing records in her bedroom. Her bedroom is her private world. When she was ten, she objected that it was too small. Her mother said, "Okay, you can knock down a wall

97

into the next room, yourself." She did, with a hammer and a crowbar. Then she repainted, spangling the ceiling with golden stars.

Now there is space for all her belongings. Her books line the walls, the entire collection of J. R. Tolkien's fantasies and many teen-age romances. She has her own TV set on which she follows soap operas. On top of the set and the bookshelves stands her collection of dolls wearing different national costumes, or representing historical figures. Henry VIII, a sixteenth-century king of England, and Anne of Cleves, one of his wives are there. So is a guard from the Tower of London in England. Some of these dolls Maria made herself.

In school, she is an excellent student. She goes to the Protestant school in Rexton; there is also a Catholic school for French-speaking children. Forty percent of New Brunswick's people are French-speaking. A third school is for Micmac Indians, one of the few Indian groups in Canada who have a reservation of their own. Some of the Indians, however, attend Maria's school, which is new, big and modern—by far the most attractive of the three.

"You have to be careful not to bump into an Indian in the corridor," says Maria, "because he'll think you did it on purpose, and he'll slam you one." In general, she is afraid of the Indians, although she makes clear that "some of them are nice." But she has never had an Indian friend and doesn't have Debbie Mosdell's appreciation of Indian problems. She knows no French Canadian children at all.

Maria is a top-notch fisherwoman, who can outdo her father at that sport any day. A favorite family story is about the time Dad caught an eel and didn't know how to get it off the hook. Maria stepped on the eel, hit its head with a rock, removed the hook and brought the eel home for supper.

She always helps cook Christmas dinner, which is shared with her uncle, aunt, family and friends. The meal has Italian accents, such as anchovy stuffing for the turkey, side dishes of artichokes stuffed with eggs and ripe olives, lots of lasagna and other kinds of pasta. The vegetable is usually greens, which Maria has frozen from the garden in the summer and cooked in the turkey stock for Christmas.

Christmas is one of the few occasions some busy Maritime families really get to eat all at the same time. This is true of the Hudson family, on Broadleaf Farms, near the village of Hopewell Hill, New Brunswick. Mr. and Mrs. Hudson, five children and nine grandchildren live on the property in several homes. They and the hired help often eat at the Hudsons', but those old enough to work are too busy tending 300 head of cattle to show up at any set hour. So Mrs. Hudson says to family, workers and friends, "Come have a meal, any time." That's exactly what they all do. A long table makes an island in the center of the kitchen—food sits ready on it—and someone is almost always having a meal.

One of them is likely to be eleven-year-old granddaughter Kim, short for Kimberley. Kim lives a fair distance away, near New Brunswick's capital, Saint John, but she spends every summer and most of her school vacations at Grandma's and Grandpa's. That's where Joker Ace, her horse, lives. Kim can't imagine life without a horse. She used to live in Ontario and had a horse there. But when she was seven, the family moved to New Brunswick. Kim sold her horse herself, to a boy her age who she felt would take good care of him. When, one Christmas morning, she found a new horse in the Broadleaf stable with a red ribbon around his neck and a card with her name on it, Kim cried.

At Broadleaf, Kim takes care of the horses her grandparents keep for summer tourists. She guides the daily tours over the softly rolling hills and through the marshlands of New Brunswick's coastal countryside. "Lots of times the people aren't used to riding," she says. "They fall off in the marshes and lose their shoes. I have to rescue them."

"Once," she recalls, "a woman lost her sweater. She didn't tell me until we were home. I had to go all the way back after it."

Kim also keeps the stable clean. She can shovel out the manure faster than any farmhand. If living with horses means coping with tourists and manure, Kim is happy to cope.

She is not only a horsewoman, she is a good softball player and a dancer, besides. She has taken dancing lessons since she was five and her training has won her an array of awards in dance contests; ten trophies, four medals, one ribbon and two cups. Grandma has some of Kim's honors on display at the farm; the rest are perched on shelves in Kim's bedroom at home, between books on the care and training of horses. Her bedroom walls are plastered with pictures of horses.

The Hudsons are not only hard at work raising cattle; they also raise silver foxes—besides taking in summer boarders and offering horseback rides—besides renting out a hall in back of the house. (They built the hall, equipped with a kitchen and small stage, to rent for local functions.)

When the whole family works together as the Hudsons do, each member takes on a share at an early age. Such sharing makes a long day shorter. Even when work is not the main issue however, members of Maritime families tend to live close to each other, sometimes in the same house. Older people may move in with married children, or nieces or nephews. There's a phrase observers of family customs use to describe this way of life: the extended family. The extended family is a rule in the Maritimes, but it's also a fairly common situation in all the Canadian provinces.

Another common situation is foster care for children. Every province takes special pains to find good homes for children whose parents aren't able to look after them. Thanks to the welcoming nature of many Canadian families, finding such homes doesn't seem to be a problem. Foster children are never treated like boarders. They are loved, watched over, punished, praised and rewarded, the same as the sons and daughters of the families where they are placed. They become their sisters and brothers. They don't have to be afraid of being booted from one home to another. Foster care usually lasts until boys and girls are old enough to be on their own.

Cindy Wylie, fifteen, is a foster child who has grown up with neighbors of the Hudsons' since she was seven months old. Cindy, whose nickname is "Smiley," because of her grin, has won her share of trophies for track and fields sports. She was also chosen queen at school in a contest for talent and attitude. Her talent is singing, which she practices daily, for herself and for her roles in the school choir. The attitude that won her a crown is her ability to be a good friend to others.

Her job at home is helping to clean house and she enjoys it. "I like the shine when I finish," she says. She wants to sing for a living when she grows up, but if she can't do that, she'll settle for being a mechanic. Tests in school show that she's gifted in that direction and she's already very clever at repairs on farm machinery.

Sometimes, of an evening, Cindy, Kim, and other boys and girls from around Hopewell go down to fish or buy others' catches in one of the bore canals. A bore is sea water traveling in a hurry up rivers and streams that empty into a bay. In bays that narrow sharply toward shore, incoming tide slaps into outflowing river water, causing friction. Slowed by the friction, the tide forms a wall of water that tears inland like a flood. New Brunswick's biggest bore is in the Bay of Fundy, but smaller bores are twice daily occurrences all along the coast.

To prevent wide scale flooding, the province has built canals into which the water can flow, with gates that open when the canals are brim full. When these gates are lifted, the water pours out as fast as it tore in. If this happens in early evening, the fishing is really great. So great, in fact, that the fishermen don't even need rods, reels, or bait. They simply let pots with sieve bottoms, attached to ropes, down into the outswooshing stream. They haul up continuous potsful of fish.

Mostly teen-age boys, and a few girls, do the fishing. People in the know go down to the bridge at gate-lifting time and buy the catch as fast as the buckets come up. The boys make good money and the customers get a cheaper meal than they could buy in the markets. The bore is a boon.

The marshland it creates also produces food. Kim and Cindy often gather wild cranberries there, and fiddleheads, marsh greens that are something like spinach, but more succulent. Marshland is good grazing for cattle too. Some of the Hudson cattle graze in one of the sections the province has set aside for that purpose. The grazing fee is very small.

Like the Hudsons of New Brunswick, the Matheson family in Nova Scotia, just across the Bay of Fundy, are cattle farmers. They live near enough to the coast for fourteen-year-old Isla Lee, who pronounces her name Ilee, and her ten-year-old sister, Lianne, to swim in summer. Their father divides his time between the cattle and a gasoline station in the town of Tagamouche, about twenty-three miles away, where he's the branch manager for a gas company.

Their mother milks the cow reserved for the family and churns butter from the cream. Lianne is in charge of caring for the chickens and gathering the eggs, for which there's a steady stream of customers. Lianne does a good job. The eggs are huge and rich, with yolks as thick as whipped cream colored with gold. Ilee manages the vegetable garden.

The family eats well: beef from their own cattle, pork and ham from a neighbor's pigs, homegrown, homebaked beans, vegetables from their garden, including much yellow turnip, popular in the Maritimes. Then there's pie from their back-yard rhubarb, and Mrs. Matheson's delectable baking powder biscuits and puffy, chewy bran muffins, laden with fresh butter. Ilee and Lianne drown their cereal and the summer berries they pick with cream that's almost solid.

They eat four meals a day. Especially in summer, when Ilee is helping to mind the cows and bring in the hay, along with her garden chores and doing the family ironing, she's ready to eat any time. Mrs. Matheson makes breakfast, dinner at noon, supper which is as big as dinner, and "lunch" which is a bedtime snack favored in the Maritimes. Summer supper is early, about 5:30 P.M., so as to allow time for more outdoor work while light lasts.

In between these hearty meals, Ilee will eat as many chocolate bars as she can afford to buy. But she doesn't gain weight, because she works and plays so hard. She fishes during the trout season in spring and brings in some whoppers. In summer, when haying is over, she rides her pony, Trigger.

For a week she goes to basketball camp. She's an agile basketball player and good at baseball, too. She pays her own way at camp from money she has earned baby-sitting, thirteen hundred dollars so far. She dips into these savings for camp, and some other pleasures like chocolate bars, but most is being saved for college.

Lianne, Ilee's sister also saves money. In Truro, a nearby city, she can get forty cents a dozen for return bottles. The summer she was nine, she managed to collect fifty dozen. The twenty dollars went into a piggy bank for spending money on the week's vacation, usually to the United States, that the family takes every year.

Lianne's favorite subject in school is English. When she grows up, she wants to write stories "especially for children." She has notebooks full of stories she writes to amuse herself. Here is one:

AN EMAGINARY (sic) CAREER

One Saturday, Mom wanted me to go and get a job. I answered back, "Why, I don't want to."

"Well, it's either that, or you won't have very much money."

"Ok, I'll see you around five. 'By."

I looked until three and I found a TV station that wanted an actress and I agreed.

I tried it for two months, but I found it was too much work. Show business isn't everything!

It seems that Lianne would rather raise the chickens for which she has won a Girl Guide badge, or collect bottles! Lianne is a homebody who doesn't like to be long away from her family. Ilee is the opposite. After college she would like to travel, "but always come home to Nova Scotia. We have everything here. From the land. From the streams. If we need something else, there's a city near enough." This is how she feels about her life.

Like Maria Connors, Ilee likes soap operas on TV. She sees more of it during vacations, because her mother restricts TV watching on school days. Children don't kick about these limits, because all their friends are in the same boat. Most Canadian parents clamp down firmly on dosages of TV.

Also, like Maria, Ilee is a steady reader, borrowing her books from the school library. She's a member of the student committee that helps catalogue and clean the books and takes turns at the desk, checking books in and out. On desk duty, between customers, she crochets doilies and scarves for presents or for sale.

Her best friend, Michelle Muëller, lives on a pig farm three miles down the road. That's where the Mathesons get their fine ham. Michelle's mother is Québecoise, her father German. Michelle is the oldest of four: there's Monique, thirteen, Heidi, nine and Jason, five. Since both parents work, Michelle and Monique pretty much manage the house and farm. Monique's in charge of the house, Michelle of the farm. Neither one could do the other's job. Once, when Michelle tried to mop the kitchen floor, she fell over the bucket. When Monique had to feed the pigs, she was dumbfounded by a barn faucet. Michelle, serving on the library committee with Ilee, had had to stay late in school. She phoned her sister. "Turn the barn faucet on over the trough," she instructed. "Come back to the phone and tell me when you've done it. I'll wait."

Monique came back. "Which way do you turn it on?" she asked.

Monique and Michelle help each other out in several ways, each sticking to what she can do best. Monique is a whiz with the sewing machine. When Michelle had to make a dress as a home economics assignment, she paid Monique to do it. Monique pays Michelle for help with her math assignments.

When the Muëller parents visit relatives in Germany, or travel on business, Michelle is left in complete charge of the farm. She collects twenty dollars a day for this work. One weekend when her parents were in Québec, all one hundred pigs and piglets broke down the pen fences and escaped. Michelle had to chase, find and capture the lot. She demanded extra pay for handling this emergency. Her parents agreed. She got one hundred dollars for the three days. Like Ilee, she's saving for college.

In the summer, Michelle and Ilee swim together when they can find time. The sand on Nova Scotia beaches is the color of the soil, a reddish brown. The beach they use, long and deep, and well maintained by the county, is popular with families for miles around. They bring their children, from tots to teen-agers, and of course beach chairs, coolers full of drinks and food, baby carriages, towels, beachballs—all the equipment that goes with a trip to the shore. To reach the water, they walk perhaps a quarter of a mile from the parking lot, on boardwalks leading through marshland and up and down grassy hillocks. Overlooking the beach are shaded picnic tables. Nowhere is there any litter. Littering is a no-no that Canadian boys and girls learn very early from their parents. Loving the outdoors, most Canadians try to be at least as clean as nature is.

When Michelle and Ilee have staked out their spot on the beach, they run to the water, splashing over sandbars and mudflats until they are in deep enough to swim. They swim hard, fighting the chill. Then they return to their spot for sunning and talking, building sand castles as they exchange confidences.

Their conversation has special accents and expressions, some of which can be heard only in Nova Scotia, or only in the Maritimes, and some of which are universal in English-speaking provinces. "I went *oot aboot* three," says Ilee, meaning she went out about three. "Oot" for out is heard coast to coast.

"Good you got oot that early, ye-es?" Michelle replies. The slow, two syllable yes, is a sort of thinking over a situation, or sometimes making a judgment. Munching on a "whoopie pie," a chocolate cookie with marshmallow stuffing, Ilee decides, "Good, ye-es."

"Like another, would you?" she offers the bag to Michelle. The "would you" isn't a question. She knows Michelle wants another. It's just a manner of speaking. Sometimes the "would you" turns into "did you," like "Caught all those pigs, did you!" In this case the "did you" is an exclamation.

In Newfoundland, one short syllable, "hah," is used instead of any one of the other three. In New Brunswick and much of English speaking Canada, the "hah" becomes "eh." Maria, describing her massacre of the eel says, "I bashed the head, eh." Eh is stuck into Canadian sentences as often as the "you know" in the United States. But with different effect. All these various short tuck-ins give Canadian speech a staccato rhythm like the subtle beat of a delicate baton on a drum.

The Mathesons' and Muëllers' southern part of Nova Scotia is entirely different from Cape Breton in the north.

Cape Breton, an island connected with the rest of the province by a long causeway, is one mountain after another, descending to the sea. The coast is bitten by stark, surf-lashed promontories. Only in summer are their summits softened by meadows of purple lupine, yellow primrose, daisies and bluebells.

Inland sprawls a series of salt lakes, the Bras d'Or, golden arms. Enclosed by hills that fold into each other before tumbling into pink sandstone cliffs, the Bras d'Or have with good reason been named among the most beautiful lakes in the world.

Cape Breton has always been a land of the sea and seafaring folk. In recent years, a semigovernment agency, the Cape Breton Development Corporation, has been encouraging other means of earning money, principally the production for sale of handicrafts long practiced at home for pleasure. Arts such as weaving and jewelry-making have in many cases been handed down from Scottish ancestors who settled in this part of the province in the nineteenth century. The corporation has also helped attract tourists and promoted some industry, including coal mines in the north. But mainly the Cape people remain attached to their sea.

Today descendants of the Scots have been joined by seafarers from other lands. Among these are the Van Schaicks from the Netherlands. In summer, they use their two motor launches, the *Eastwind* and the *Seawolf* to transport tourists through the Bras d'Or to rocky islands in the open Atlantic where wild birds nest.

The skippers for these trips are Peter Van Schaick, twelve, and Vincent, fourteen. They have five older brothers and sisters living nearby, so the family is always together holidays, and as often in between as possible. They enjoy working and playing together. When the parents had a twenty-fifth anniversary, all the children gave them a winter trip to the warm Caribbean Islands, a welcome escape from Cape Breton's northern blasts of wind and snow.

In summer, the family runs a small cottage resort, which everybody helps keep in sparkling shape. Peter also has the special tasks of minding the milk cow, the bull and the chickens. He sells the eggs.

He and his brother are the joint owners of a huge piece of driftwood, which stands on four legs on their lawn, looking for all the world like a well-antlered deer. In fact, when the boys went to drag it from the lake, they thought they were going to save a drowning deer. Close-up, they discovered their mistake, but decided the wood was worth hauling in.

A trip to the bird islands can be rough; the sea around Cape Breton sometimes kicks up mightily. But both Vincent and Peter are expert pilots; they handle a boat with the easy confidence that comes from long familiarity with the temper of local waters. Vincent is also a skilled handyman with boat repairs. When he graduates from high school he plans to enter the Coast Guard College at Port Edward in Cape Breton. The sea will be his career.

A sailor's life is not for Peter, however. Peter's special interest is math in which he has earned a collection of honors from school. He wants to use it to become an architect. The two boys are different in many ways. When their parents took them to the Netherlands to visit grandparents, Peter thought the trip was super. He hopes to go again. Not Vincent. "Too rushed," he said. Cape Breton is a quiet place.

As a mountainous island, and as a province of seafarers, Cape Breton has something in common with Newfoundland, the Maritime to the north. There, however, the resemblance ends. The Maritimes are the least well off for money of all the Canadian provinces, but Newfoundland is the least well off even of those. That's why the Emberley family in Rushoon, whom you met at the start of this book, cook on a wood stove with wood they gather themselves, instead of on their electric stove. The shiny-clean electric stove is hardly ever used, because electricity is just too expensive.

The Québec-governed section of the Labrador-Newfoundland province has plenty of cheap electricity produced from Québec's roaring rivers, but the English-speaking sections can't get their hands on it, because of the boundary dispute between the two provinces.

So the Emberleys cut wood. Father chops and Mother, Ivan and Joanne strip bark from the trunks. One trunk was saved for the mast of their boat. Father bought an old hull; Mother made the sails. They use the boat for fishing and picnics on islands in the bay off Rushoon. They never come home from a picnic without a load of driftwood. The driftwood adds to the fuel supply for cooking and heating, and, fortunately, can be gathered in summer. Forest wood has to be cut in winter because stinging black flies are so thick in the summertime forest.

Of course, fish is brought home from the picnic too. Much of the picnic catches, the leavings Mother gets from her job at the fish processing plant and the occasional hauls Father makes is either salted, pickled or dried for winter fare. Both Ivan and Joanne hate fish. Their response to it is "Yuk!" They prefer chicken and chips, a Newfoundland fast food favorite. But they eat what they hate. That's what there is.

The Emberleys didn't always live in Rushoon. They came from an island off the coast, something like Fogo. There was only a one-room schoolhouse for the children and no medical service at all. The government offered to relocate the people, paid for the moving and helped them to get a new start. The Emberleys took advantage of the offer.

The school the children go to now is big, but barracks-like. Both Joanne and Ivan are good students and Joanne is a top athlete besides. The little living room in the Emberley home is jam-packed with her trophies. She's also a 4-H club leader who is looked up to by younger children in the community. She has been a baby-sitter for many of them.

She hopes to earn enough baby-sitting money to pay her way in a school that will train her for work in a beauty parlor. That's her choice for the future. But although she already does all her girlfriends' hair, the future seems dim to her because she's so occupied right now with chores in the house.

The women of Newfoundland are the mainstays of their families. They are usually equal wage earners with their men; often enough, they are the main wage earners. And since there's a home to run at the same time, household responsibility is early shared with girls like Joanne. Mrs. Emberley works in the fish processing plant from about five-thirty in the afternoon until about one-thirty in the morning. So, Joanne must do what her mother can't.

However, Joanne's future might be easier than she thinks. The off-shore oil discovery may make it possible for Newfoundlanders to earn much higher incomes than at present. In that case, Newfoundland would no longer need the help the rest of the country grudgingly now gives the province. Canadians of more fortunate provinces tend to sharpen their tongues when speaking of Newfoundland. They make unpleasant jokes about "Newfies," a name Newfoundlanders deeply resent. There are even comic books about "Newfies." Offshore oil could change all this, provided Canada can decide to whom it belongs.

Meanwhile, not everybody in Newfoundland has to struggle. There are families who live very comfortably in the suburbs of Saint John's, the island capital. Toby Rabinowitz's family is one of these. Toby's father is a professor of child psychology at Newfoundland's Memorial University. Her mother, a childhood education specialist, teaches in Saint John's.

Toby, ten, and her two younger brothers, live in a spacious home on a hilltop above Portugal Cove, a small outport a few miles from the city. Toby has a great many friends in the neighborhood and in the outport below. After school, they generally gather at her house, because it's the biggest and her mother's cookies are the best. Toby takes piano lessons and is passing on what she learns to several of her group. The sound of music fills the house almost every afternoon.

If the weather's bad, another sound is added: fast pattering feet jumping rope. Usually, the jumping is outdoors, but it's allowed inside when there's no other way. The rope artists have dozens of songs they sing and recite, which contain instructions in jump rope language for the motions to be performed. Every so often someone brings a new combination of steps, which is tried out and worked on like a ballet rehearsal. Here is one of the fanciest:

> Spanish dancers do the split, split, split.
> (*The jumper performs three splits over the rope*).
> Spanish dancers do the kick, kick, kick.
> (*The jumper hops with one foot, kicks with the other*).

*St. John's, Newfoundland,
nestles among the
rocks of the harbor.*

Spanish dancers do the round, round, round.
(The jumper makes a circular swing over the rope).
Spanish dancers get out of town, town, town.
(The jumper leaps off the rope with both feet).

Some days, Toby and her pals gather around her piano for a good Newfoundland sing. They all know the rhythmic folk songs of the province, most of which, like this one about Jack, the sailor, tell tall tales about fishing and the sea.

The truth about a fisherman's life is never as comical as Jack's story. The father of one of Toby's friends lost a five thousand dollar catch when his dump truck opened on the way to the processing plant and the entire load slithered down one of Newfoundland's near-vertical cliffside roads. The whole family, children included, spent the night cleaning off the road. Toby's friend didn't feel much like singing or jumping rope the next day.

Besides teaching music, Toby gardens. She grows an assortment of vegetables, but her speciality is strawberries. She sells strawberry plants for thirty cents apiece, sometimes as many as 300 in a season.

She is thinking about trying to sell some of the ceramic work and stone sculptures she does as a hobby. That will make the money for the new bike mount faster. Like all Canadian children, even in families that don't have to worry about money, Toby is expected to work and save for her special needs and desires. Work is as customary a part of growing up as play.

Boys and girls who live in Saint John's, rather than out of the city, like Toby, have a problem finding a place to play. The green, henna, turquoise, blue and teal-colored clapboard houses of Saint John's are packed one up against the next,

JACK THE SAILOR

Now 'twas twen - ty - five or thir - ty years since
Jack first saw the light. He came in - to this world of woe one
dark and storm-y night. He was born on board his fath-er's ship as
she was ly - ing to 'Bout twen-ty-five or thir - ty miles south-

CHORUS

east of Bac-ca-lieu. Jack was ev-'ry inch a sail - or,
five and twen-ty years a whal - er, Jack was ev-'ry inch a
sail - or. He was born up-on the bright blue sea.

When Jack grew up to be a man, he went to the Labrador.
He fished in Indian Harbour, where his father fished before.
On his returning in the fog, he met a heavy gale,
And Jack was swept into the sea and swallowed by a whale.

REPEAT CHORUS.

The whale went straight for Baffin's Bay, about ninety knots an hour.
And every time he'd blow a spray he'd send it in a shower.
"O, now," says Jack unto himself, "I must see what he's about."
He caught the whale all by the tail and turned him inside out.

REPEAT CHORUS.

fronting on tiny sidewalks. Except around a few stately old homes with gables and bay windows, which have been broken up into apartments, there aren't any yards. Children solve the problem by using the streets.

The streets aren't set officially aside as play streets; children and traffic share them. Basketball nets are attached to the sides of houses; courts are marked off with chalk. Drivers do their best not to interrupt the progress of the street games.

Most of the games are ball games of one sort or another, and most of the players are boys. However, city girls use the streets for the same kind of jump rope games Toby plays. They have to jump on the slant, because Saint John's is so hilly. About the only level street is along the harbor, and that's much too cluttered with the business of loading and unloading huge freighters to allow for play. Jump rope in their city takes strong muscles and strong will.

CHAPTER **8**

Mid-Canada: Families of Ontario and the Prairies

CANADIAN CITIES STILL CLAIM THE GREATER PART OF THE country's population, but with increasingly fewer children. Families with children want to give them the freedom of the open air in a land that offers so much of it. So more and more of them are moving to suburbs or rural areas.

The Ojas of Ontario are an example. They moved with their two boys and two girls from the city of Sault Saint Marie in Ontario to the country, where they are raising goats. The oldest boy, Eric, is now out on his own, but Liisa, fourteen, Mark, fifteen, and Stephanie, six, are all doing their special things on a farm called Pond-R-Oja.

The name is a reference to the four ponds on the property, the long *pondering* over the move, plus the family name, Oja, which comes from Finnish grandparents. The family pets, Sinikki, the dog, Aiti Kessa, the cat, Meeko Linto, the canary, all have Finnish names. So does Liisa's horse, Sasha.

A cattle round-up on the northern prairie.

Besides which, count a dozen ducks, as many rabbits, and of course, the bank account animals—the goat herd.

Liisa's special thing is Sasha, her horse, a gift from Grandpa. To earn money for Sasha's feed and care, including the proper shots from the veterinarian, Liisa minds neighbors' goats when they are away. She had to make friends with fifteen guardian dogs before she could get near the herd. Growling, they nipped at her heels, and jumped at her hands, but finally calmed down as she stood still and talked to them.

Liisa boards Sasha up the road a piece from Pond-R-Oja, with family friends, who have a stableful of horses. She and Maria Adamson, the neighbors' daughter, ride together as often as the weather and their chores allow. They ride anywhere they please, through fields, up hill and down. When, that is, Liisa can make Sasha go where *she* pleases, instead of where Sasha decides. Sasha had never been mounted until Liisa took the reins. Liisa is breaking her in slowly: meanwhile every ride is a toss-up between Liisa's will and Sasha's.

Liisa will win. Willowy-slim, blonde, with a flashing smile, she looks more like a model than a horse-trainer or a goat-herder. But her cover-girl looks are deceptive. She is as determined to tame Sasha as she was to tame the neighbors', dogs.

As horses are her special thing, so her brother Mark's specialty is cars. He built himself a motorized go-cart for driving around the Oja farm. Repairing automobiles, both engines and bodies, earned him the money for go-cart parts. He intends to be an auto mechanic and body worker when he graduates from school. Summers, he also earns money as an evening disc jockey for a roller skating rink in the nearest town, Bruce Mines. A gifted accordion player, he and a friend who's equally good with a guitar sometimes get paying engagements at local parties. Between parties, they practice and play for pleasure.

Mark and Liisa each receive ten dollars weekly for helping with chores. Liisa does the kitchen cleanup after every meal, sets and clears the table, helps cook. Mark works with the goats and rabbits. Both wash dishes, Mark one week, Liisa the next.

Little Stephanie feeds the ducks. Stephanie was a foster child in the Oja's care until they adopted her. Stephanie was born with a handicap called Down's Syndrome, which makes her act like a three-year-old at the age of six. But thanks to patient training by the Oja parents and the love of the whole family, Stephanie behaves like a very advanced three-year-old. Mark and Liisa, and Eric, when he visits home, treat Stephanie a bit like a pet. They play with her, hug her, give her goodies. When she was christened, relatives and friends from near and far came to the ceremony and the party afterward. Stephanie had a lot of thank you's to say for all the presents she received. In spite of presents and petting, Stephanie isn't spoiled. She has her duck chore. She takes her own dishes off the table. She is being brought up, as far as possible, just as her brothers and sister were.

Brother Eric, sixteen, lives with the local postman and his wife. He helps deliver mail after school and during vacations, paying board from his salary. He and his parents don't get on. They don't approve of his smoking or his swearing. Four letter words are no-no's in the Oja family, as in almost all prairie households. Prairie people are very strict about children's behavior, but no more so than about their own. Most of them are active church members, usually of the United Church, which is a union of former Methodist, Congregational, and some Presbyterian churches. For this group, what the Bible says is not just for Sundays.

Eric isn't against the church; just, for the time being, against anybody telling him what not to do. He's sad about his family's disapproval of his life-style. "We just don't understand each other," he says, "so I guess it's better I live away." He comes home often, helping with the goats on his visits.

Goat raising has setbacks and advantages. When the Ojas' prize doe, the best milker of the herd, rolled over and died, the setback was severe. The Ojas hoped some of her brood would inherit her large milking capacity. Not only were these hopes dashed, but there was fear other goats might catch what killed her. She died on a holiday when the local veterinarian's office was closed, so the Ojas couldn't take the dead animal for an autopsy. Only cutting her open would determine what had been the matter. So they stowed her in the freezer overnight. They didn't sleep too well. Worry kept them restless. Luckily, when the autopsy was done, they found the goat didn't have a disease that could infect the rest of the herd.

One of the advantages of goat raising is the prizes a good herd like the Ojas' can win in agricultural fairs, or "aggies," as they are called. Such fairs are common summertime events in Ontario and the prairie provinces. As a rule, they are just what their name suggests: a show-off place for animals, fruits, and vegetables, along with farm women's handwork, such as doilies, quilts, bedspreads, clothing. There's always a section for animals and crops raised by boys and girls, and the girls' handwork, too. The children's exhibits are usually sponsored by 4-H clubs.

Sometimes horseshows and horseback riding contests are

part of the fun, along with horse pulls. In a pull, the horses drag loads of bricks or steel from a starting point to a goal. Of course there is plenty of homemade food for sale and often a big barbecue. But rarely are there any merry-go-rounds, ferris wheels, or games of chance. The aggies are farm festivals and what farming families bring is sufficient to make them festive.

At the Goat Keepers' Field Day in the region where the Ojas live, six different kinds of cheese, ice cream, yogurt, brownies, fudge and butter, all made from goats' milk, are offered for sampling and for sale. Boys and girls stuff on the samples.

Goats' milk, which is all the Ojas ever drink, has a rich texture and a touch of salt flavor. The Oja children think cows' milk is blah. Compared to goats' milk, it is. Goat cheese clings to the roof of the mouth the way peanut butter does, until the full flavor, whether mild, sharp, or middling, has been savored. The Ojas plan on opening a plant in Bruce Mines for the manufacture of cheese and other products from goats' milk. The plant will have a dairy bar for snacking and take-out.

The aggies where the Ojas show off their goats compete with parades for the summertime crowds of Ontario and the prairies. Which are more popular is hard to say, but music gives parades an edge. Ta-ta-rah, ta-ta-rah, ta-ta-rah, here come musicians like Mark, high-stepping ahead of pony carts, flower-bedecked bikes, costumed riders on prancing horses, floats of all descriptions. There needn't be a special occasion for these parades. All that's necessary is for a few people to get together and decide, "Let's have a fun day." The few enlist another few and soon a parade forms. When Sasha's trained, Liisa will be parading her.

The parade is followed by sports contests between towns. Every town gets wind of the nearest town's fun day and attends, each, of course, rooting for its own team. After the games, there's apt to be dancing in the streets. Summer fun days are a distinctive, joyful, mid-Canada happening.

Christmas, of course, is another joy, Canada-wide. But in central Canada the preparation is half the fun. At the Ojas, preparations start early in November. Mark, Liisa, Eric and Stephanie study the Sears Roebuck catalogue so hard the pages turn flimsy. Their parents do the same. Finally, each person picks the one most-wanted present. Then comes name-drawing day. A bowl, containing the names of all family members and the presents they hope for is passed around. Everybody draws a slip. Father Oja takes the children, one by one, to the Sears Roebuck store in Sault Saint Marie to buy the present for the name each drew. After the shopping, the two have dinner at whatever restaurant the gift-buyer selects.

In big families, and especially extended families with many cousins, uncles and aunts, the custom provides for everybody to receive a gift, yet nobody is burdened with having to give more than one. And the drawing is always exciting.

At the Ojas, after all the presents have been opened on the big day, there's a big dinner. One of two meats are served as the main course: stuffed raccoon or stuffed rabbit. Raccoon takes long, slow and careful cooking, but when roasted as Mrs. Oja knows how, it's a rich, luscious dish that gets calls for seconds from everybody who isn't as stuffed as the raccoon. The rabbit, faster cooking, is more delicate. The Ojas can eat thirds on rabbit.

Like the Ojas, the Myers, who live outside the village of Claremont, Ontario, came from the city to give their children, Darren, twelve, and Robert—"Robbie"—nine, a country life. They moved from Toronto, the province's biggest city. Mr. Myer still drives there to his work. Mrs. Myer also drives in to her part-time job.

The Claremont area was once farmland, and although some farmers remain, it has become more and more a community of families like the Myers. Both parents are willing to take the commuting in order to let their boys grow up in broad fields instead of streets or small lots.

No way, in Toronto, could Darren have built the A-frame tree house where he and his friends sometimes camp for the night. To reach it, they shinny up a neighboring tree, then swing across a horizontal rope. If thirst attacks, Darren siphons water through a plastic tube from a plastic tank at the bottom of the tree. The tree house is his own, his particular property.

On the broad, sloping lawn below the house, he and his brother have their catapult, a forked pole, tall and flexible, with a tin can containing a rock, secured in the fork. To fly the rock, the boys bend the pole over and let go. The rock arcs into the distance. The object is to see who can send the rock farthest.

Their catapult is modeled on a weapon ancient Romans used in warfare. Their father helped them put it up and helped build the tree house, too. He spends a great deal of time with the boys after work. When weather keeps them inside, he makes puzzles for them from wire coat hangers. Robbie has become so clever at untangling the woven wire that he can do it blindfolded.

Darren sometimes fancies himself as an imaginary strong man, named Conan, who lived in an imaginary time, twelve thousand years ago, called the Hiborian Age. Conan is the redheaded hero of a series of books by Robert E. Howard.

Darren likes to curl up with the Conan stories, also with J. R. Tolkien's books about the Hobbits.

He likes to ride his five-speed bike, too. He and Robbie both have five-speeders with all the extras, including speedometers. Their parents gave them half the money to buy the bikes; they had to earn the other half. One way they earn money is raising and selling pumpkins. They do a brisk business around Halloween.

Like all Canadian children, they are expected to do many things for themselves. When they decided they wanted embankments for their electric train set, their parents said, "Fine, you make them." They did. They rescued styrofoam packages brought home from the supermarket until they had enough to mold into embankments.

Early in the morning on school days, they fill their own lunch boxes, choosing, within limits, what they want to take. Their mother watches. When they return from school, ravenous, they raid the refrigerator for their own afternoon snacks, mostly raw vegetables and sliced meat for sandwiches. Maybe a cookie. Mother frowns on starch and too many sweets. A single exception is the fudge Robbie makes. It's apt to come out so hard, the boys have to break it up with a hammer. They throw out more than they eat.

Boys and girls who live in Toronto where the Myers came from, take to the lakes for their freedom. Toronto is Ontario's biggest city. Luckily, it's on Lake Ontario, which also borders the American state of New York. Georgian Bay, part of Lake Huron, which touches Michigan, lies to the north. Their shores are dotted with summer cottages. Almost every family who can afford a cottage or a cabin, has one.

In the city itself, a good many neighbors have indoor and

outdoor swimming pools with lessons for children. The city operates playing fields for football and soccer. There are centers where boys and girls can study photography, painting and ballet, or practice gymnastics. They can visit exhibits and see shows put on specially for them. If a fee is charged, chances are they can earn money with a newspaper delivery route. They pile homemade go-carts with their wares and trot house to house, before and after school. The rattle of go-cart wheels is a familiar sound in Toronto's residential sections.

Still, according to Gregory—"Greg"—Watson, fifteen, city life is "tame." Greg lives in West Toronto, a pleasant community of snug private homes, but he would rather be closer to nature. On Lake Ontario, where the family has a cottage and a boat, he swims, sails and water-skis. At a friend's place on Georgian Bay, he chops trees, makes rafts and sails them. He brings some wood home to Toronto for the family fireplace.

He especially remembers one piece of action on Lake Ontario. He and his father were caught in a sudden squall. They had a struggle hauling down the wind-tossed sails. When they succeeded, the motor wouldn't start. The boat was keeling at a forty-five degree angle when they finally got the motor chugging and were able to pull into a cove.

Conquering a squall, sailing a raft, hewing wood, these add up to Greg's idea of really living. Meanwhile, he collects old jalopies, repairs them and puts them on the road. He buys old stereos and makes them good as new. Sometimes he can sell what he remodels, but mostly the remodeling is for pleasure. To pay for parts, he cuts lawns and repairs cars in the neighborhood. Like Mark Oja, he intends to be an auto mechanic or engineer when he grows up.

Boys and girls who grow up in the prairie provinces of

Manitoba and Saskatchewan don't complain about any lack of challenge. For most of them the quality of life depends on grain and how much their fathers can get for it.

The Bjornson farmhouse in Manitoba is a history of good crop years. Twelve-year-old Julianna and ten-year-old Valdine Bjornson, whom you met in the first chapter of this book, practice on a piano paid for by lentils. A good lentil crop also paid for a shower, and a bumper wheat harvest decorated the dining room. A triumph with trefoil covered the cost of a modern kitchen. Trefoil is a kind of clover, used as cattle-feed. Admire Valdine's and Julianna's house and you are admiring their grain fields.

Success hasn't come easily to the family. "Barney" Bjornson and his brother, who lives across the road, bought fifteen hundred stony acres of bushland. They couldn't afford machinery to clear it. They dug out rocks and roots by hand, until, discouraged by the endlessness of the job, they decided to quit clearing until they could earn money to rent machinery.

They went to work cutting wood on Hecla Island, some miles away, in Lake Winnipeg. They cut in the dead of winter, because summer had to be reserved for planting and harvesting land already cleared. Crisscrossing the logs on sleds mounted on skis, they hauled them over the frozen lake with the help of their one piece of machinery, a tractor. Behind the sleds came the caboose they had built to live in while gathering the wood.

The hauling was a tricky business. Extreme cold often split the ice, which contracted again in treacherous ridges. Snowfalls hid the damage. Unless Barney could detect the faulty spots, his loads were in danger of sinking. One evening the danger came so close he had to unhitch the whole train.

127

The sleds were dragged by hand, one at a time, across the ice. That was a long winter's night.

There was another long night on the mainland when his tractor sank in mud. In the Lake Winnipeg section of Manitoba, prairie fields are ditched for draining into the lake. At convenient points, hay is sunk into them, with logs on top, to provide crossings. A crossing Barney was using collapsed. He worked until four o'clock in the morning trying to pull his tractor out of the ditch. When he slashed his hand open in the effort, he gave up, temporarily. Next afternoon, he and his brother returned to rescue the machine.

Thirty-four years after such trials, Barney Bjornson says, "I never felt badly off, even though we had almost no money and had to get help from the bank, so we were always in the hole. You see, I had hopes, I had dreams." He looks around the fine kitchen his trefoil bought. "Now I have everything I hoped for, all I dreamed of."

What he has achieved is so precious to him that he doesn't like to leave it. Friends ask: "Don't you ever take a vacation?" He answers, "I *am* on vacation."

Valdine, Julianna and their mother do persuade him, however, to take them on occasional vacations: to visit relatives who settled in the American state of Minnesota and to drive around Lake Winnipeg. On the lake drive, they spend the night at a lodge run by Indians.

The girls know the lake's Hecla Island very well, but not the way their father and mother knew it before they were born. Hecla has become a provincial park. The Bjornsons and all their relatives have anniversary parties at a resort inn there. When the girls look at the movies their mother took of life in the caboose and the woods on Hecla during the logging operations, they can hardly believe it's the same island where the family now parties and Valdine camps with her school class.

One of the girls' great summertime pleasures is driving with their mother (Father's too busy in the fields) to the city of Winnipeg for the yearly folk festival. There, they watch the ethnic groups of Manitoba perform their special dances and hear them sing their special songs. Best of all, the girls sample all the special foods on sale at the many booths. When Valdine and Julianna play with their Barbie dolls, they sometimes pretend to take them to the old-time Russian, or Ukrainian, or Icelandic, or German, or French, or Scandinavian, or Mennonite, or you-name-it booths to taste the goodies cooks have been concocting for days.

The Mennonite booths are among their favorites. The Mennonites are a religious group who started in Switzerland, spread through central Europe, then to North America. They live in colonies of their own, preferring to keep apart from others.

Many such colonies of religious sects, founded mostly by Europeans, are scattered thoughout mid-Canada. The annual folk festival in Winnipeg, Manitoba, is a fine place to get acquainted with a variety of them.

To families of Saskatchewan, Manitoba's western neigh bor, grain is as important as it is to the Bjornsons. Bruce and Brian Mann, eleven-year-old twins, and their sisters, Gail, fourteen, and Heather, nine, live on a Saskatchewan farm about 100 miles out of the capital city, Regina. The four young Manns go to school in Grenfell, a nearby small town. How many days they can go in winter is a question, which depends on whether Dad, who runs the local snow plow,

129

can clear the road of the mountainous prairie drifts. The school year begins in mid-August, because the likelihood of lost days, when even the toughest plow can't shove the snow, is so great. Sometimes a blizzard whistles through while children are in school. No way can they reach home. They stay in the town's blizzard shelter until the storm subsides.

The Manns have a way of being sure when storms of any kind are coming. The children's horses, Blondie, Candy, Scamp and Star, head for the barn. Candy leads the others, because she's an expert latch-lifter and lock-picker. She lifts the latches on the corral gates, undoes the locks, and ushers the other three to shelter. If she wants extra oats, she slips out by herself and lopes, whinnying, up to the house.

For a while the Manns had an Indian foster son, Calford, who was an expert with the horses. He rode as if he and the horse were one. But Calford was restless. He had never known that children could grow up in just one home. His alcoholic parents had been unable to care for him and other relatives hadn't either. He had run from every family where he had been placed. Picked up on the streets of Regina, he was welcomed by the Manns, who tried hard to help him. But Calford's damage was deeper than they could repair.

One day when he and Brian were fooling with some other boys, Brian told one of them to shut up. Calford thought Brian was speaking to him. He felt insulted and took off. The Manns grieved over Calford and the four children couldn't understand why he left. The whole history of the Canadian Indian was back of his run.

From time to time, the family whisks into Grenfell. Gail roller skates at the rink there and Heather borrows every book about animals that comes into the public library. Mrs. Mann does some shopping while the children visit Grandma, who lives in town. For major buying, however, the family makes the 200-mile round trip to Regina.

Grenfell, like all prairie towns, is flat, and in summer hot and dusty. Towns are laid out in precisely measured blocks, with avenues running east and west, streets running north and south. Most streets and avenues have numbers instead of names, though occasionally one may be named after another Canadian town or province, or perhaps a famous Canadian. Big cities follow this pattern, too. The layout simplifies finding one's way about. Except when one-way streets force a detour, the Manns have no problem arriving quickly at the locations they need in Regina. That's important when a family must drive 200 miles for tractor parts, clothing and groceries.

The Manns buy as little store food as possible. Bruce raises chickens and collects the eggs. The family sells what eggs they don't need, which aren't many, because the children eat nonstop. Along about eleven in the morning, their mother says, "No more breakfast till dinner." She bakes five loaves of bread three or four times a week, sometimes oftener, along with cookies, cakes and pies. The family favorite is Saskatoon pie, made from their own berries. Saskatoon berries, plump and purple, taste like a cross between a blueberry and a currant. They grow in all the prairie provinces, on bushes almost as tall as trees.

None of the Mann children is allowed junk food. There are no potato chips or other crunchies in the house. But they can nibble all the homegrown fruit and vegetables, all the home-baked pie, bread and cookies they please. They do. Constantly.

Gail is the athlete of the family. She is pitcher or left fielder on her school's all-girl baseball team. The team has a

131

record of winning eight out of ten games a year played with other schools, including boys' teams. Gail gets a lot of satisfaction out of beating the boys.

Her life is far from being all play, however. The Manns grow flax—important for its oil, which is used in paint—and wheat. The prairies produce two kinds of wheat—durum, for making macaroni and other pasta, and hard wheat for bread flour. Sometimes the Manns also grow barley and rapes. Edible oil comes from the rapes. These grains, along with rye, are the major source of prairie family income.

Whole families must work together to provide the care these cash crops require. May is seed time and June is weed time. Seeding is done with a disc; weeds are sprayed. The July schedule may be lighter, but August can keep a family harvesting the fields until one or two in the morning. When the Mann children were little, Grandma stayed with them during harvest, while their parents worked the swather and the combine. Now the children help, too.

A swather cuts the grain stalks and piles them in rows. A combine, with ten different parts, first cuts the grain from the stalks, then separates the chaff, or straw, from the grain. A part called an auger sucks the cleaned grain into an elevator that lifts it to a storage tank. Other parts spew out the straw. A second augur showers the grain into the farm granary. The combine looks like a prehistoric monster, lumbering and snorting around the S-shaped curves in which the cropland is contoured.

When the grain is ready for harvest, the prairies are a picture. The fields wave in multihues of gold: greenish, amber, orange. Like a patchwork quilt, they stretch as far as the eye can see. Here and there, on a slight mound, a circular clump

132

of trees interrupts the quilting, but trees are few and far between. Prairieland is open to the gilding of the sun.

The only tall objects, reaching so high that they can be sighted from miles away, are the white towers of the grain elevators. There are twenty-three hundred of them in Saskatchewan alone. To these, farmers bring their harvest for sale. The rectangular towers are double, a small one on top of a big one, each with a two-sided, sloping roof. Inside are the bins into which grain is elevated after being weighed and graded. Railroad tracks come to the base of the towers. Grain is poured into the cars that will carry it to market.

How much per load will the Mann family be paid for the grain they deliver to the elevators? The amount depends on many factors. The two most important are the weather and the Canadian Wheat Board.

The Wheat Board sets the price the elevators pay and limits the number of bushels a farmer is allowed to produce on each acre. The limit prevents glutting the market. A glut is an oversupply. An oversupply causes a severe drop in prices and consequently a severe drop in what farmers can earn. The Board also tries to take some of the guesswork out of farm income through a subsidy fund, on which Mr. Mann can draw if prices drop below a certain level. The Board contributes two dollars per bushel to this fund and Mr. Mann contributes one dollar. The subsidy is a cooperative venture between farmers and the Board.

Mr. Mann must also contribute to the operating costs of the Wheat Board and the elevator where he takes his harvest. Sometimes the elevator is too chock-full to accept what he brings. Then he has to keep it in his own granary. If he grows more than his quota, he has to store the extra, too. He can receive advance pay on the store, but the advance will be deducted from his next year's pay. If he has sufficient space, and if the weather stays dry, storage is not a great problem. But in rainy weather, bugs infest the granary. He has to fumigate—another expense.

Rain is both a hazard and a blessing. Without enough, crops shrivel and die. But rain between swathing and combining time will make wheat sprout. Sprouted wheat earns less money. "You have to guess the weather, eh, and hope you're right," Mr. Mann sums up. "Farming is a real gamble."

Of course the Manns have their highs as well as their lows. Good years bring good money. The official money period for farmers is from July 31st of one year to August 1st of the next. If grain prices rise during that time every farmer gets a share of the increase. If they go down, the subsidy helps. Christmas stockings for children are leaner or plumper, depending on grain prices. During a price rise year, the Christmas stockings at the Mann farm are full to bursting.

Alberta, Saskatchewan's neighboring province to the west, is less dependent on grain. It has long been famous for its beef. Large cattle ranges stretch across the south, tended by cowboys. Dozens of horse and cattle shows star the summer calendar, along with some exciting stampedes and rodeos. But since the discovery of oil in Alberta in the 1960s, farmers have begun to see more money in gushers than in cow pastures. The cattle business is declining. The capital, Edmonton, once a town of boardwalks pitted by cowboy spurs, is now a city of high-rise condominiums, thanks to oil money. And the money is likely to last. Alberta has one of the greatest oil reserves so far known in the world.

The Taylor family, who lives not far from Chauvin, are in cattle country and they stick to their herds. John Taylor, thirteen, wants to be a cattle farmer like his father when he grows up. His ten-year-old sister, Janice—"Jan"—is into horses. She has won forty-seven 4-H ribbons for those she has raised. No wonder. She spends hours grooming them. Her Christmas list always includes hook picks and brushes along with saddles and bridles. She won her first ribbon when she was only three.

John raises some of the family herds himself. At fairs he almost always wins a first prize for his results. What he likes best, however, is driving the tractor. It's air-conditioned and has a radio!

His 4-H club started him on his hobby, pheasants. He raises them not to eat or sell, but to protect them from coyotes and hunters while they are young. Pheasants are not yet an endangered species in Alberta, but he is afraid they may be soon. They are becoming fewer.

Early in June, 4-H gives him a batch of chicks, along with feed. John adds oversized turnips and radishes to the feed for them to peck on. Otherwise the little ones would peck each other half to death. He keeps the brood in a pheasant house until August. Then he moves them to a halfway pen, a preparation for wild life. He fills the pen with bush to imitate field and forest. The pen is roofless, so the birds can make trial flights. In due time, the pheasants fly off for good. Some will perish, but far fewer than those who are raised without protection.

On top of pheasants, cattle and horse care, John and Jan tend the vegetable garden and pick the berry crop. Like the Manns, their favorite berry is the Saskatoon. Jan also likes peas, especially raw peas. She eats steadily while she picks. When her mother asks, "Where are the rest?" Jan pats her stomach.

Now and then John and Jan take an afternoon off to visit

with Martha, Miriam and Paul, their friends in a nearby Hutterite settlement. The Hutterites, whose ancestors came from Switzerland, are a prominent religious sect in the prairies. Their rules forbid boys and girls from leaving their settlement to play with outsiders, but they like outsiders to come play with them.

Martha and Miriam live with their mother in the women's and girls' part of the settlement. Paul lives with his father in the men's and boys' part. Families live in apartments, segregated by sex. Their apartments have no showers or bathtubs. There's a common bathing hall, with separate sections for the sexes. There's a common dining room, too, but men and women eat at separate tables. Boys and girls have a wing of the dining room, boys in one part, girls in the other.

The Hutterites have their own style of dressing. They make all their own clothes. Martha and Miriam wear long skirts and a bodice buttoned over a white or yellow blouse. Clothing is always buttoned or hooked. Zippers aren't allowed. Nor are women and girls allowed to walk around with their heads uncovered. Miriam covers hers with a black kerchief, polka-dotted in white. Underneath the kerchief, Miriam parts her hair in the middle, from forehead to the nape of her neck, and again from ear to ear. She combs the front sections forward and rolls them in a semicircle. She does her back hair up in a bun. Martha does her hair the same way.

Their little sister braids her hair tightly around her head and plops a white cap on top to hold it in place. Not until she's ten can she don a kerchief and do her hair like Miriam's and Martha's.

Brother Paul wears black pants, held up with suspenders, and usually a white shirt, though he may wear a sport shirt for farm work. His hair is cut short. His father dresses the same way and his mother dresses like Miriam and Martha. Their hairdos and clothing styles are part of their religion. Their names come from the Bible.

Among themselves, families speak a German dialect, but the children all learn perfect English in their Hutterite school. The school is strict, and so are parents. They thrash their children with a strap for the slightest misbehavior—even an accidental spilling of milk.

As soon as boys and girls are old enough, they work alongside their parents to raise and prepare food for the whole settlement, with enough extra to sell for the common bank account. No individual Hutterite owns anything except clothes. Everything else belongs to everybody and everybody has to work. Miriam, Martha, and other girls take care of geese, ducks, poultry and pigs. They milk cows, pick vegetables and help freeze them for winter eating. They prepare meals and clean up afterward side by side with their mothers.

Paul and his father plow, harrow, plant, harvest, raise cattle, build homes and barns, erect fences, put up and repair all the community structures. They also make elegant furniture. Women and girls do fancy needlework. They are very skillful seamstresses.

John and Jan Taylor especially like to visit the colony when hot loaves of bread are ready to lift from the ovens. They know they will be offered a slice. Hutterite women sell some of their baked goods and their needlework. Their husbands sell some of the furniture. The money goes to buy supplies.

Much as they enjoy visiting, however, John and Jan wouldn't care to live like Miriam, Martha and Paul. They don't envy the endless hours of work. Not that they don't have to work, themselves, but much of what they do is their own

Martha and Miriam at the
Hutterite settlement near
Chauvin, Alberta.

choice. The highlight of their year, the March-to-November horse and cattle shows, is a good example. The Taylors miss very few of these. Before and after a show, work is double, preparing and catching up. "We help our parents because they help us," John explains.

The day before departure, there's barely time to talk. The cattle truck and horse trailer are made ready. The family camper is packed with all the necessities except the food Mrs. Taylor has been cooking for the last two days. At six the next morning, the food, the cattle and the horses are loaded, and off the Taylors drive with high hopes of winning prizes. "Even when we don't win," says Jan, "we have a lot of fun."

Once a year, Jan, John and their parents put aside thoughts of cattle and horses to camp with friends in the Rocky Mountains of northern Alberta. They travel in a cavalcade of camper trucks. Once, counting neighbors and relatives, there were seventy-five of them. Their favorite camping ground is near broad and tranquil Lake Louise, where the boys and girls canoe and row. The lake is the color of a milky sapphire. The blue comes from melted glaciers and the milkiness from silt they dislodge as they grind their way down from the peaks that encircle the lake.

Camping is almost as necessary to many, if not most, Canadians as the roof over their heads. It's a national habit, and fortunately well-equipped campsites abound, making the urge to get away from the house and "oot" with leafy trees for a roof easy to satisfy. No matter how little or how much a family earns, no matter if home is in the city or a suburb or already in the country, come summertime, camping calls. There's only one answer: yes.

CHAPTER 9

A Good Life
on the Pacific Coast

JOANNA GOULD, TWELVE, HER BROTHER MATTHEW, TEN, AND sister Helen, fifteen, sail with their parents every summer to some of the islands that fringe the coast of British Columbia. They desert their large suburban home, the trampoline in the back yard, and the neighbor's swimming pool, for tents. They carry their tents, back-pack other gear, and travel on ferries, which ply from island to island. When they tire of one island, they hop a ferry to the next. Island-hopping is a high point of their summer, even though they camp elsewhere, too.

They have driven in a rented trailer to the Grand Coulee Dam in the state of Washington, and to Disneyland in California. Sometimes relatives from England and Wales join them on such trips. Then they visit the Goulds at home for a while. The Goulds, in turn, visit them.

Once, the Goulds were dramatically surprised by a relative's arrival. On a Christmas Eve, a red-suited, white-haired,

The city of Vancouver lies between the mountains and the sea on Canada's west coast.

white-bearded Santa, with a pack of presents, rang their door-bell. On removal of wig and beard, he turned out to be an uncle from Australia.

Children of the Goulds' relatives add to the large group of neighborhood boys and girls who play in the Gould yard and in the ravine below the house. The trampoline, of course, is a great attraction. In hot weather, the children wet it down with a hose, so that when they jump, they get a shower bath. Matthew likes to bounce the others unexpectedly. He jumps, and the trampoline throws them into the air. Being unpre-pared, they don't usually come down on their feet—more likely on their fannies.

Jump rope on the trampoline is a favorite game. With practice, girls learn to turn somersaults over the rope. One of Joanna's best friends, Tiina is expert at this. She and her brother Tiimo, are Finnish. Every other summer they fly to Finland to visit relatives.

Most of the boys and girls in the neighborhood are accustomed to travel. When they come home, they show each other pictures taken on their trips. They have a lot of stories to exchange.

Their special meeting place is the Gould children's club house, built in a tree down the ravine. To become a club member, a boy or girl must pass tests on the trampoline, in the swimming pool and in running. Members share the work of keeping their clubhouse clean and tidy. Anyone who messes it up, or behaves badly, is expelled for however long the club decides is necessary.

Approaching their hideaway, boys and girls keep a sharp eye out for snakes in the tangled undergrowth. They don't mind too much sharing the ravine with the snakes. Watching for them is an adventure. "Besides," says Joanna, "they're a sort of protection for our club, too."

At the bottom of the ravine is a narrow-gauge railroad track, over which a tourist sight-seeing train clacks by twice daily. It's called the *Royal Hudson*: royal, because it once transported British monarchs. A few other small trains also jerk along the track, tooting like the locomotives of a toy train set. Matthew and Joanna put pennies on the tracks, so the trains can flatten them.

All the neighborhood boys and girls know the spots where the tracks cross the road. They know the *Royal Hudson's* schedule, too. They go down to the crossings at the right hour to wave to the engineer. He waves back and makes his whistle wail.

In summer, when not scrambling down the ravine or performing acrobatics on the trampoline, Matthew, Joanna and Helen swim in their neighbor's pool. They and their friends play a game in the water called *Marco Polo*. The person who's "it" is blindfolded. When he yells, "Marco," the others must answer "Polo." From the sound of their voices, he tries to determine their whereabouts and tag one of them. If he suspects that a swimmer has climbed poolside, he hollers, "Fish out of water." If, indeed, a player is out instead of in, he becomes it. Otherwise, a tagged person is the next it.

Sometimes the children's father plays the game with them. He's such a big man that the children slip easily out of his way. Matthew, especially, delights in swimming silently close to him, then slipping off under water. Matthew is also an expert diver for pennies, another sport the pool crowd enjoys.

The Gould bike-jump is Matthew's creation. He built

it by piling up bricks and slanting a board slab of plywood from the top of the brick pile to the ground. Starting at some distance from the jump, he pedals to maximum speed, glides over the plywood and flies through the air to the ground on the other side.

All three of the young Goulds are athletic. They were the first in their area to win the cross-country running award, which is given for running 300 kilometers, the Canadian distance measurement, within one year's time. That's about 180 miles.

Helen and Matthew have swimming awards; Joanna is the sailor. She belongs to a sailing club for boys and girls, where she takes lessons. Her dream is to have a boat of her own.

Helen, according to her sister and brother, dreams about boys. The three children have their own rumpus room in the basement, on one wall of which they have painted, printed and carved a twenty-four feet long and eight feet high mural representing their pet ideas, and plastered with their favorite sayings. Helen's liking for boys is described on the mural by Matthew and Joanna in this couplet:

"If all boys lived across the sea,
  What a swimmer Helen Gould would be."

The rumpus room gets heavy use in winter. It's where the children play their favorite indoor games, Scrabble and chess, look at TV and listen to stereo. But only *after* homework. As in the majority of Canadian families, the law is homework first.

In the winter outdoors, Joanna, Matthew and Helen ski cross-country and slide on inflated inner tubes. They mound up snow to make jumps. The winter high is, of course,

Christmas. Stockings are hung at the end of each bed, to be opened whenever the children awake. But the main presents are delayed until after they have washed the breakfast dishes and cleaned up the kitchen. Matthew usually eats two breakfasts, but Christmas morning, he's quite content with one!

The Christmas tree stands outside in a pot. Red, white and green streamers loop through the dining room. Helen's and Joanna's Paddington bears wear Santa Claus hats. They hang their stockings too, but all they get inside is tinsel. The Paddington bear is the hero of a series of books for boys and girls. The Goulds have all these books. The books and the bears were gifts from their English relatives.

To Christmas shop, and on other shopping tours, the Gould children drive with their mother into the center of Vancouver. They are always glad to leave the city.

Children who live there though, don't necessarily feel citified. Vancouver is a city of neighborhoods, each with its own schools, shops, playgrounds. These are the children's world.

Not that they are cooped up in their communities. When they have reason, they traverse the city. Though David, John, —"D.J." —Walker, and his pal, Kevin Gee, whom you met together in the first chapter of this book, live some distance apart in Vancouver, they have no trouble getting together weekends.

D.J.'s home is a spacious, terraced apartment in a building his father owns. His room is a museum of souvenirs from Panama and Costa Rica, where he lived when he was little. His father is an engineer, so the family has lived in many parts of the world. When D.J. was eight, the family returned to Canada and set up housekeeping in Montréal. D.J. immediately went in for hockey. When the Walkers moved to British Columbia, D.J. had to learn the game all over again. The rules in the west of Canada differ from those in the east. Kevin, whose father manages a team in the hockey school where D.J. enrolled, helped D.J. learn the western way.

While he was learning, D.J. felt put down whenever his team lost a game. Now he is less tense. "Hockey is like life," he philosophizes. "You train. You work. Then you take what comes."

For D.J. hockey *is* life and will be for as long as he can play. He intends to become a pro. But he's going to a university first. "When I'm too old for the game, I'll need the education to do something else." This is point of view he arrived at from the books by hockey stars.

In the years he has attended hockey school and hockey summer camp, and the hours he spends practicing alone on a field across the street from his home, his skills have grown steadily. They have earned him shelves full of medals and trophies. Quite likely, he *will* become a star, maybe playing the fence, which is his position, on a team that wins the world championship Stanley cup. That would quiet all his doubts! But if not, he will have the background to follow other interests.

One such interest now is his foreign coin collection. Besides coins he collected in Panama and Costa Rica, he has bought coins from nine other countries. He's a canny buyer, knowing what shops have good offerings at reasonable prices. He collects stamps, too, and matchbooks. One of these days he is going to run out of space to store all his treasures. A special one is a set of Chinese stamps Kevin gave him.

The first time D.J. had dinner at Kevin's house, he had a few minutes' trouble mastering chopsticks. But it took only those few minutes for Kevin to show him how easy they really are to handle. And they are ideal for lifting the chunks and shreds and slices combined in Chinese dishes.

Picking up rice wasn't all that easy. "Hold the bowl near your mouth," advised Kevin, "but not too near." Sticking one's nose in the bowl is considered very bad manners. "And never," Kevin warns, "try chopsticks on Jello."

Chinese families celebrate many special occasions and plentiful food always marks the celebration. On the Chinese New Year, at Christmas, at the Harvest Moon festival, when a baby is born, or when other happy events occur, eating is a principal occupation.

The exact date of the Chinese New Year varies, because it depends on phases of the moon, but usually the holiday arrives in February. A parade of paper dragons prances through the streets of Vancouver, and in other cities with Chinese populations. Bystanders set off firecrackers. Then everybody goes home and eats. The Autumn Harvest Moon festival features moon cakes as part of the meal. No matter what the occasion, each person will find a *lisee* in his rice.

Lisees are little red envelopes bearing pictures of boats, fish, lanterns—whatever an artist thinks attractive. At the harvest festival, they contain money, supposedly to feed the gods in thanks for crops. Most of the time, however, they hold just good luck sayings, drawn in Chinese characters. At New Year's, the lisee in a bowl of rice is intended to bring luck for the whole year—provided every grain is eaten. Lisee or not, there's little danger of any being left.

While these big meals are being prepared in family kitchens, the children play games. Kevin and his teen-age cousins, Teri, Tami and Deanna Lee and Alan Mak usually play Mah Jong, chess, poker, or some other card game. In the Lee family, Tami, who is a good pastry cook, often makes

147

the dessert ahead of time. Her mother relies on her for the moon cakes at the Harvest meal.

The Lees have a big house, so many of the family gatherings are held there. To cross the yard, people walk on stepping stones engraved with Chinese characters copied from coins used in four dynasties of ancient Chinese rulers. Before mounting the steps, they must cross a small bridge, arching over a pool. The outside of the Lee house could be a set for a movie about old-time China. The inside is thoroughly modern.

In the summertime, the whole family—Kevin, his parents, his cousins and his uncles and his aunts—go fishing or camping. Among them, they own several boats, on which they may spend four or five days at a time. Now and then, they sail up the coast to a spot where they have cabins.

Kevin especially likes to drive to the lakes of the Okanagan region east of Vancouver. The Gees, the Lees and the Maks try to arrive there when the peach crop is ripe. They return with bushelsful loaded in their cars. The Walkers do the same thing. In peach time the Okanagan valley is invaded by British Columbians who know how delicious those fresh-picked peaches can be. The fruit is shipped all across Canada, but traveling coast to coast, it loses flavor and gains cost with every mile.

The Okanagan Valley has a lot to offer camping families, besides peaches. There's a desert to explore, mountains to climb. Children particularly like climbing among the Voodoos, cliffs that have been eroded into ghostly faces and figures that are blushing under the sunset, eerie under the moon.

Sometimes the Gees' and the Lees' and the Maks' summer camping gives way to travel, mostly in South America, California or Mexico. But the next trip the Gees take will be different. They are going to spend a month in mainland China. Kevin is curious about what it's really like.

Kevin's father is a chemical technologist. His specialty is research on adhesives. Mrs. Gee is an admitting clerk in a hospital. Both parents work hard. Mr. Gee makes the next-day lunch sandwiches for the family at midnight and Mrs. Gee is up at six in the morning and on her way to work.

Still, they save time for Kevin. On her hours off, his mother watches his progress in the rink where he takes his figure-skating lessons. His school homework is inspected. His manners are corrected. Most Chinese parents feel a deep sense of obligation to their children. The Gees are no exception to this rule, though they do sigh a bit over the one hundred dollar a pair cost of ice skates for his growing feet.

What do the Gees have in common with all the different sorts of families in which Canadian boys and girls are growing up? Where do they fit into the bouquet of other backgrounds from which Canadians come?

And how about contrasts in life-styles created by mountain fastnesses, flat plains, seacoasts, cities, Arctic tundra, lush orchards? Can Kevin have anything in common with boys his age in Québec or Newfoundland; or his cousin, Tami, with girls of the prairies?

The answer is, yes, indeed. Canadian boys and girls who take part in the country's interprovincial exchanges feel quickly at home in the families with whom they stay. Here are the reasons why.

Practically all children are expected to work and save money. Practically no children are allowed to watch television without parents' consent. Nor are they allowed much snacking of other than homemade foods. Homework is a must.

Kevin Gee and his cousins at a family celebration.

Sports are a big part of life. Winning prizes is important. Reading is encouraged. Being polite is vital.

Love is everywhere. The "generation gap"—parents and children not understanding each other—is rare. Family lives are like a piece of weaving in which the whole depends on each thread. The threads don't go off in different directions. Parents and children work, play, plan, travel together. Furthermore, the interwoven life is a very wide piece of tapestry. Boys and girls grow up, for the most part, among large circles of affectionate relatives.

This is not to say that Canadians are one big happy family. Well cared-for Kevin, for example, couldn't easily understand the behavior of an Indian boy whose parents were too drunk to raise him properly. The plight of the Indian is a sorry fester on Canadian life, and the bitter quarrels between provinces are other sores.

But every country in the world has wounds in its fabric. Just possibly, Canadian boys and girls, with more in common than they yet know, can one day heal the wounds in theirs. They have the spirit for any dare.

Bibliography

The acknowledgments listed in the front of this book are its real bibliography, since the contents are mainly based on live research in the field. However, the following technical documents and reference materials were also consulted:

Annuaire du Québec, 1980-1981. Ministère de l'Industrie et du Commerce, Bureau de la Statistique du Québec: Québec, 59ᵉ édition, 1981.

The Canadian Constitution, Publications Canada, Ottawa, Ontario, 1981.

L'École Secondaire Louis Riel. La Commission des Ecoles Catholique de Montréal, Québec, 1973.

Education Canada: Secondary School Student Exchanges. Canadian Bureau for International Education: Ottawa, Ontario, 1980.

Explorer's Guide. Government of the Northwest Territories, Yellowknife, 1980.

English, L.E.F. *Historic Newfoundland.* Newfoundland Department of Tourism: Saint John's, Newfoundland, 1975.

Holbrook, Sabra. *The French Founders of North America and Their Heritage.* Atheneum: New York, 1976.

Inuvik, A Canadian Development in Modern Arctic Living. Inuvik Research Laboratory, 1980.

Honigman, Irma and John J. *L'Enfance des Esquimaux de Frobisher Bay.* AINC Publication No. AS-0006-051-FT-A-14, 1979.

Kelly, Tom, *Canada Today.* Vol. VII. No. 7. Canadian Embassy, Public Affairs Division: Washington, D.C., September, 1976. Note: *Canada Today* is a free monthly publication which may be useful to social studies classes. Each issue deals with a different aspect of Canadian life and is written by different authors, qualified to discuss the given subject. The above cited issue, for example, dealt with the life of children. Others cover such topics as art and architecture, economics, education, etc. The address for subscriptions: Canadian Embassy, Public Affairs Division, 1771 N. Street, N.W., Washington, D.C. 20036.

Job Transfers Can Affect Your Children's Education. Wright, Bunny, in *Skyworld*, July, 1980.

Koring, Paul, ed. *Canada North Almanac.* Research Institute of Northern Canada, Yellowknife, 1977.

North of '60, The Eskimos/Inuit of Canada, Information Canada, Ottawa, Ontario, 1974.

Northern Indians. Inuvik Research Laboratory, 1980.

Our Family, Family Newspaper of the Anglican Diocese of the Arctic. Vol. VI, No. 1, April, 1980.

Malcolm, Andrew H. *Canada's Native Peoples. The New York Times,* Sept. 1, 1980.

———, *For Trudeau, the West Is Not Yet Won. The New York Times,* August 10, 1980.

Oil and Gas, Are We Ready? Report of a Conference sponsored by the Extension Service of the Memorial University of Newfoundland, October 23-26, 1979.

An Overview of Canadian Education. Grayfer, Margaret, Canadian Education Association, Toronto, Ontario, 1978.

Pile Construction in Permafrost. Inuvik Research Laboratory, 1980.

Programmes Voyages-Échanges. La Commission des Écoles Catholiques du Québec, Québec, 1979.

Reindeer Herding. Inuvik Research Laboratory, 1979.

The Renewable Resource. Forest Information Service Division, Ministry of Forests, Victoria, British Columbia, May, 1971.

Rural Living. Saskatchewan Tourism and Renewable Resources, Regina, Saskatchewan, 1980.

Saskatchewan Notes. Government of Saskatchewan Information Services, Regina, Saskatchewan, 1980.

Index

156

page ii—(facing title) Canadian Consulate General; 17—
Canadian Consulate General; 29—National Film Board of
Canada (photo by C. Lund); 43—NFB Phototheque (photo
by Dunkin Bancroft); 57—Canadian Consulate General; 74—
Canadian Government Office of Tourism; 92—Canadian Gov-
ernment Office of Tourism; 113—National Film Board of
Canada; 140—Carlson, Rockey & Associates.

DATE			

© THE BAKER & TAYLOR CO.